The Complete
Illustrated Guide to
Numerology
★★★★★

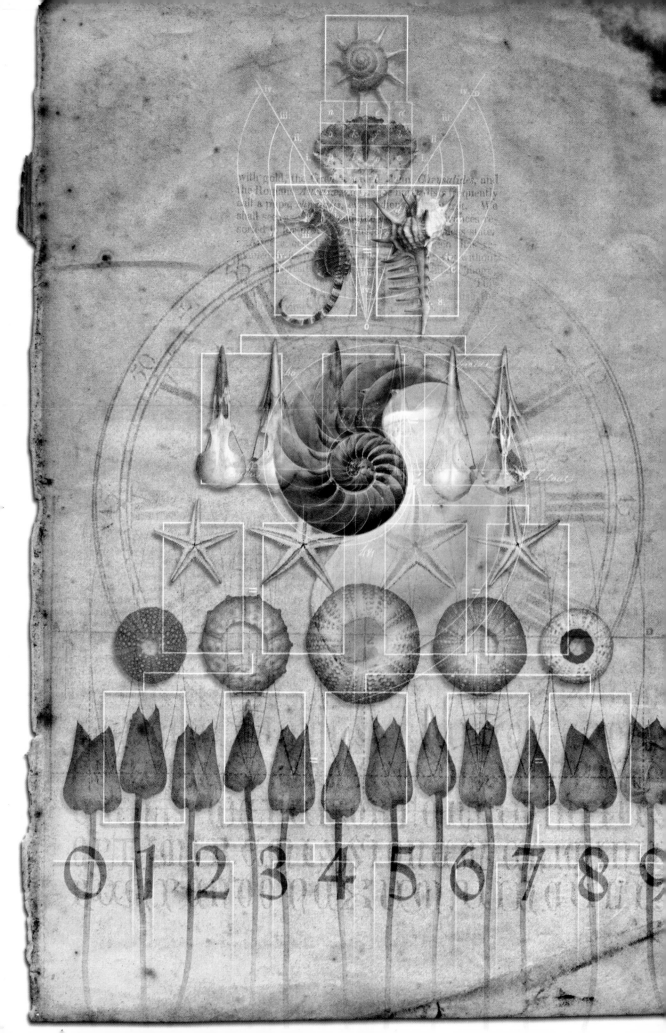

with gold, the *Greeks* name it the *Chrysalides*, and the *Romans* *Aureliæ*, because they are frequently call a *majestic* brightness, as a *golden* light. We shall see...

The Complete
Illustrated Guide to
Numerology

★★★★★

SONIA DUCIE, AIN

ELEMENT

Shaftesbury, Dorset • Boston, Massachusetts • Melbourne, Victoria

First published in Great Britain in 1999 by
ELEMENT BOOKS LIMITED
Shaftesbury, Dorset, SP7 8BP

Published in the USA in 1999 by
ELEMENT BOOKS INC
160 North Washington Street, Boston, MA 02114

Published in Australia in 1999 by
ELEMENT BOOKS
and distributed by Penguin Australia Ltd
487 Maroondah Highway, Ringwood, Victoria 3134

Designed and created for Element Books with
The Bridgewater Book Company Limited

ELEMENT BOOKS LIMITED
Editorial Director Sue Hook
Managing Editor Miranda Spicer
Project Editor Kate John
Group Production Director Clare Armstrong
Production Manager Stephanie Raggett

THE BRIDGEWATER BOOK COMPANY
Art Director Michael Whitehead
Designer Jane Lanaway
Editorial Director Fiona Biggs
Managing Editor Anne Townley
Editor Sarah Bragginton
DTP Designer Chris Lanaway
Illustrators Ron Cavedaschi, Richard Constable,
Nicola Evans, Sharon Harmer, Catherine McIntyre
and Caroline Seatory
Three dimensional models Mark Jamieson
Photography Mike Hemsley SIBP at Walter Gardner
Picture Research Liz Moore

Printed and bound in Italy.

British Library Cataloguing in Publication
data available

ISBN 1 86204 568 2

The publishers would like to thank the following
for use of pictures:
Berenice Benjelloun pp. 69, 84, 126, 141, 173, 179, 181;
The Bridgeman Art Library pp. 10, 30, 65, 90, 141, 170, 182–3; Corbis pp. 89, 145, 175; Liz Eddison pp. 140, 141;
e.t. archive p. 56–7; Hulton Getty p. 181; Image Bank pp. 102, 103, 121, 132, 133, Science and Society Picture Library pp. 144–5;
Tony Stone pp. 9, 11, 17, 24, 25, 26, 27, 28, 36, 37, 38, 40, 41, 42, 43, 45, 64, 68, 70, 71, 73, 76, 77, 80, 82, 98, 99, 100, 101, 103,
105, 109, 114, 117, 119, 120, 123, 124–5, 128, 130, 131, 134, 135, 137, 138, 139, 140, 142, 143, 152,
154–5, 156, 158, 159, 161, 162, 165, 168, 169, 171, 172, 174, 176, 181.

ACKNOWLEDGEMENTS
A very big THANK YOU to Element MD Julia McCutchen, publicists Jenny Carradice and Tierney Fox, and to my agent
Teresa Chris. A warm thank you also to everyone involved in the design, illustration, and production of this book. Sonia.

CONTENTS

* * * * * * * * * * * * * * * * *

WHAT IS NUMEROLOGY?

★ ★ ★ ★ ★

> "The Book of
> Nature is written
> in numbers"
>
> GALILEO

Numbers, it is believed, were first used before words. Modern scientists and archeologists studying the ancient world have found traces of evidence to support this theory in the form of notches carved on wood and stones, and primitive forms of the abacus (a system used for counting). Numbers have always been teaching people about life.

To a Numerologist, numbers are representatives of nature that can expand your mind and offer philosophical, psychological, and scientific insights on life. Numbers can be interpreted as energies or vibrations, constantly changing and adapting to the world they represent.

You can discover the power of numbers in your own life, from matters of the heart, your work, or other areas of everyday life. Equally, you can see the world at large through art, music, science, and literature. By applying your logical mind and your inner wisdom to interpret numbers, you can develop your intuition. Numerology can help you to understand what can be gained from your journey through life and inspire you to unravel its inner mysteries.

ABOVE Italian astronomer, mathematician, and physicist Galileo, 1564–1642, recognized the significance of numerology.

DISCOVER LIFE'S RHYTHMS
THROUGH NUMEROLOGY

* * * * * * * * * * * * * * * * * *

LIFE IS MADE of a series of interconnecting situations and circumstances, and each moment and each situation leads you on to the next, linked by a thread of consciousness inherent in all life – mineral, vegetable, animal, and human. Energy pulsates through creation. It may sound odd to say that a carrot possesses a string of consciousness, but it was created by nature, and the energy from the sun enabled it to flourish and grow.

Numbers have consciousness too, as they represent the inner or hidden energies contained within life on earth (and the universe) reflected through the outer experiences they portray. All of life's potential is represented in the simple numbers 1 to 9, which can be seen working in your life by observing your own personal numerology chart, drawn up from your date of birth and your names. For example, if you are facing a certain situation, then you may find an explanation in your chart, which may also indicate lessons you may learn from the experience. Numerology can also help you to understand more about the bigger picture in life, such as world situations that affect everyone's lives.

Life is a mirroring process, and numbers can reveal true meanings and offer you information to help you with your life. Like attracts like; if your Personality Number is a 4, you may find that you draw people to you who can teach you about the qualities contained within this number, for example. If you are in a 6 Personal Year (a number which changes with each birthday), you may attract to you lots of love and affection (qualities of the 6), or perhaps you may allow people to walk all over you at times (another aspect of the 6).

Numbers are cycles that repeat themselves, and each number cycle between 1 to 9 highlights strengths, challenges, and potential in every area of (your) life. The earth travels around the sun over and over again, the oceans ebb and flow, the moon travels through cycles that influence even the crops that are grown. Your body is born and you then experience the ritual of each age (1, 2, 3, 4, 5, 6, 7, 8, 9) and in the spring, summer, fall, and winter of your life. Everything in life has its time, and your body has natural highs and lows. This is the chain of evolution, and these cycles can be identified by applying numerology.

Each number cycle, like each day, flows into the next, which means that at times you can be influenced by the previous or following numbers in your chart. Each number cycle, 1 to 9, contains potential physical, emotional, mental, and spiritual elements, which can allow you to identify your own personal rhythm in life. When you are at one with your own rhythm, then your life simply flows, but it is difficult to be in tune all of the time. External stresses play a significant role in altering your rhythms as you try to conform to the demands which the outer world places upon you, whether from time stress, work stress, relationship stress, or health stress.

Numerology can help you to manage stress: as new situations, demands, and responsibilities come into your life, take a step back and learn from your numerology chart what life is teaching you and how best to manage your life. It may also be that some of the stresses in your life are of your own making and therefore numerology can bring to your awareness the need to take personal responsibility.

ABOVE Numbers relay important information – we make so many calculations at home, at work, and in everyday living.

Even periods of disruption to your natural rhythms, occasions when you put up a resistance to life, are essential times for growth and are still a part of the flow. For example, when you are confused you are forced to look inside yourself to question your own inner values, to make decisions, and to see the actions needed to move you forward. Numerology can help you to identify these times and to highlight lessons from the issues surrounding them. Many problems stem from the past, even though they may seem like very present concerns. As numerology mirrors what you need to learn, it can also help you to release negative patterns that may hold you back in the future. Disruption and disharmony may not seem easy to bear at first, but welcoming change can take you deeper into life and may be richly rewarding in the long run.

A GUIDE TO THIS BOOK

Numerology is a tool that allows a little knowledge to go far. You can learn about the qualities of each number in this book, but it is your intuition or your inner knowledge that guides you to interpret these numbers and apply them to your life. Numerology therefore becomes an interactive science, a personal philosophy and a fascinating psychology, making it a powerful tool of personal development that can inspire your mind, body, and spirit and can encourage you to be yourself.

Topics in this book are far-ranging, from politics to food, from complimentary therapies to economics. The compendium of information revealed by numerology allows you to cast your own interpretation upon these matters. Some topics will click, while others may not capture your imagination immediately.

While reading this book, particularly with the Personality Numbers, you will see compound numbers or double digits with a third single digit at the end. For example, if you were born on the 17th of the month then you may see it written 17/8 (i.e. 1 + 7 = 8). All these numbers influence your Personality, but the 7 has the strongest influence. The 7 and 1 flow through the number 8. In numerology the single digits 1 to 9 are the strongest because they are essences which are reduced down from larger digits, but a compound number can give you additional information as to how a specific energy is influencing your life.

Numbers are moving energies. You do not become a number, but its energy influences you. You may recognize some of the qualities associated with the numbers in your chart but others may simply remain part of the unexplored potential. Have fun, and enjoy the wonderful world of numbers.

LEFT The aftermath of an earthquake is a chilling reminder that we must learn to adapt to any given circumstance in life.

RIGHT Discovering mutual compatibility in your personal relationships is just one of the many positive aspects of numerology.

THE HISTORY OF NUMEROLOGY

* * * * * * * * * * * * * * * *

NUMEROLOGY IS A part of every culture, but some – such as the Chinese, Tibetan, Hindu, and Greek – have developed methods that are used around the world.

Each culture has developed its own form of numerology based upon its level of consciousness and collective energies. For example, in some parts of the world people spend their entire lives upon the same piece of land. Their numerological interpretation of the numbers they use in their everyday lives may be very different from those of a urban culture, particularly if they have no contact with the outer world. Perhaps these cultures see numbers as physical things: for example, 1 represents man going out to earn a living, 2 nourishes the land to grow food, 3 is active in order to maintain the land and keep it in good order.

Numbers lie at the roots of evolution and reflect back information about any society or culture they represent, as the outer world always mirrors the inner process of life. The value of numbers may remain the same, but their numerological interpretation changes according to who applies them and when. Indeed, today numbers can be counted up to billions and added up to form a single digit between 1 and 9.

ABOVE The abacus – a primitive form of calculation still used by some cultures today.

DIFFERENT NUMBER SYMBOLS

Numbers are written in different ways by the different peoples around the world. By looking at the various methods – such as Roman, Hindu, Greek, and Babylonian numbers – we can see much about these societies and cultures.

Each village, group, or society had (and still has) teachers, whose job is to record information about their group through numerology. For example, great works like the Bible, the Kabbala, and other books can be numerologically translated to provide information about the time in which they were written and the society they represented.

Numerology is also seen on great buildings. The number of steps or pillars and their shape and geometry reveal a great deal about a particular society's way of life. It is possible today to read any book or examine any building or form from the past and to access information about society or culture in its time. This is the powerful energy of numbers at play once again in everyday life. Today the great architects and builders mirror modern society and culture, so that people of the future can find out about us.

BELOW The Chinese developed their own system of numerology.

RIGHT Imagine the complex calculations and total manpower involved in the creation of the great pyramids of Egypt.

TEACHERS

Pythagoras was a Greek mathematician who possessed a brilliant mind and developed his own method of numerology, which he taught at his School of Mysteries in Italy around 600 B.C.E. His system explored the qualities of the numbers 1 to 9, but he also believed 10 to be a perfect or sacred number because in essence it contained energies of all the numbers 1 to 9.

Like many inspired teachers throughout history, it is said that he was castigated by his local community and feared for the knowledge he imparted to others.

ESOTERISM IN NUMEROLOGY

Esoteric numerology is also based on the numbers 1 to 9, but it additionally takes into consideration numbers 1 to 81 (from multiplying 9 by 9). This is an ancient method of looking at the concepts and ideas behind the numbers in order to connect with the deeper mysteries of life. Esoterists understand that all life is born out of energy and concepts or ideas, and that infinite potential is contained within them. They place the emphasis on freedom from the world of form (not in a way of denial, but of acceptance) and stress the existence of the Soul over the immediate wants and desires of the Personality.

DIVINATION

Divination is a method whereby numbers are calculated to give specific outcomes to situations in a black and white way and to offer predictions. Sometimes people receiving divination are so terrified of the prediction that their fearful thoughts contribute toward creating the situation. At other times a predictable outcome bears no relation to reality. But prediction usually contains some grain of truth.

THE KABBALA

The Kabbala is an interpretation of the Old Testament by Jewish mystics, and Gemetria is the name given to its system or method of numerology, based on the phonetic sounds of letters, which are all translated into numerological value. Names carry vibrations and some people who adhere to this system choose their names and their spelling carefully in order to maximise their influence and effect. By incorporating the phonetic sounds, Kabbalists communicate powerfully what they mean.

LEFT Greek philosopher and mathematician Pythagoras, c. 580–500 B.C.E., believed numbers to be the ultimate elements of the universe.

ABOVE Leonardo Da Vinci, 1452–1519, was a brilliant painter, sculptor, architect, engineer, and scientist: he was a genius with numbers.

Certificate of Merit

...ough in the County of Middles...

No.	When	Name of	Father's Name and Surname

1 2 3 4 5 6 7 8 9 0

Deaths since 24th April 1856

Distribution	Field Officers	Captains	Subalterns	Staff	Sergeants	Drummers	Rank & File	Totals of N.C.O. and Rank & File	All Ranks	Remarks
1st Division	13	66	115	25	26	167	4899	5257	5452	
Highland "	17	39	42	24	226	4	3490	4324	4496	
3 "	12	44	112	22	21	132	3754	4095	4428	
4 "	17	46	134	36	282	129	4815	5326	5509	
"	17	49	134	25	37	136	5526	5454	5619	
Light "	21	61	160	16	810	156	4194	5234	5514	
Total	102	260	747	148	480	727	27368	29690	50680	

PART ONE

NUMEROLOGY: THE BASICS

★ ★ ★ ★ ★

With the ever-changing world around us, our individual personalities have the potential to react in many different ways. They can be influenced by the people around us and by changing circumstances that occur at all stages of our lives.

Numbers are energies which carry within them immense possibilities. Your Personality Number reveals the patterns of behavior that stem from your childhood. Working out your numbers is one thing, but interpreting them is another. Simply allow your intuition to guide you to "read between the lines" as well as learning from the knowledge contained within

ABOVE Since earliest childhood, we have been introduced to the intriguing world of numbers.

this book. Your Personality Number alone can reveal a tremendous amount of information about your life and provide a valuable aid to personal development. Life isn't black and white, nor are the influences of the numbers. Not only can you come to understand yourself more clearly, but everyone with whom you come into contact on your journey through life.

NUMEROLOGY:
YOUR PERSONAL ORGANIZER

★★★★★★★★★★★★★★★★★★

NUMBERS ARE ALL around you. Keeping a record of those that are most significant or important can help you to observe how the overall patterns of numbers influence your life. For example, you may not think that your work telephone number is important, but this number vibration and the qualities it contains can strongly influence your life at work. Your birth certificate number is extremely significant, as it is unique to you and it influences your potential.

In order to record all these many numbers that have an effect on your existence, you could create your own Personal Organizer. It provides numerological information right at your fingertips which you can delve into whenever you like. For example, when someone new enters your life, such as a new boyfriend or girlfriend, you can discover from them their significant numbers and then look up in your fact file to see whether any of their numbers are mirrored in your personal numerology chart.

This Organizer can also be helpful when you are working through specific Personal Year vibrations. Perhaps you are influenced by a 27/9 Personal Year, for example, and you are finding many challenges to your emotions. By referring to your Personal Organizer you may find that the number 9, or the 27/9 is already in your chart, which

RIGHT Keeping a personal record of your numerological influences can help you understand more about your whole life including personal relationships.

LEFT The numbers you dial on a phone can reveal information about the people to whom you are talking.

may show you the area(s) you are working with at that specific time – such as your Personality, Life Path, or Karma Numbers.

Life moves in a whole variety of patterns and cycles, and when you begin to chart these numerologically you can interpret these cycles and patterns much more successfully. By studying all the major cycles, and the Universal or Collective world cycles, you can begin to understand more about the world in which you are living today.

Personal Organizer

	NUMBER	NUMEROLOGICAL VALUE
Day of birth *(Personality Number)*		
Whole date of birth *(Life Path Number)*		
Month number *(Collective Number)*		
Full names on birth certificate *(Karma/Wisdom Number)**		
Vowels in your full names *(Soul Number)**		
Consonants in your full names *(Childhood Number)**		
First name *(Major Goal Number)**		
Middle name*		
Other names*		
Surname *(Family Number)**		
Birth Certificate number		
Social Security number (US)		
National Insurance number (UK)		

Home Organizer

Home street number		
Home apartment number		
Home street and apartment together		
House or apartment name		
Town/city/village name		
Country name		
Zip code or Post code		
Home telephone number		
Home fax number		
Mobile telephone number		
Home e-mail number		
Vehicle registration number		

Work Organizer

Work building name		
Work building number		
Company name		
Office number		
Personal ID number/payroll number		
Health Club membership number		
Work e-mail number		

*To translate a letter into a number see page 28

PERSONALITY NUMBERS

✶ ✶ ✶ ✶ ✶ ✶ ✶ ✶ ✶ ✶ ✶ ✶ ✶ ✶ ✶ ✶ ✶

IN NUMEROLOGY YOUR Personality Number is one of the most important aspects of your chart. This is because you function from your Personality – which is like an outer garment of clothes – in the material world. Sometimes you can become preoccupied with your wants and desires of your Personality (I want that dress, I want that relationship), and it is completely human to want the things that you want. When you were a child you may have believed that you could get every little thing you wanted, but as you grew up you realized that life isn't like that. Though the saying goes "You get what you need," sometimes this is also what you want; at other times it seems your individual needs and deepest desires are far from being satisfied.

Your Personality Number highlights your psychological patterns of behavior. By becoming aware of ways in which you act and react to life on a daily basis, it can help you to accept or change patterns which hold you back. For example, you may have a 5 Personality Number influencing you; one of its patterns is that you may want to run away every time something goes wrong in your life. By being aware of this, you can say, "Oh, here I go again," and make a conscious decision about how to take positive action. Of course, you are more than likely to repeat the same patterns over and over again. Eventually, you will become aware of them. However, even when they are

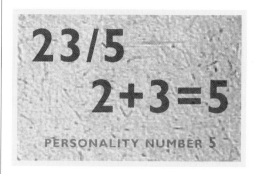

brought to your attention you may still choose to continue with your behavior.

Your Personality Number is influenced by your Life Path Number (and vice versa), which brings soul elements into your life. Your soul is your inner essence, which continues after you die and guides you through life. You may not be aware of your soul, but it is always there. In numerology your Soul Number can also help to identify some of the qualities your Soul is teaching you. Your Personality Number interacts with all the numbers in your chart, but your Life Path Number and Personality Number have a special relationship because they work very closely together to provide many of your life experiences.

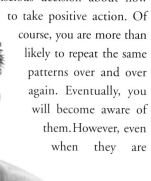

CALCULATING YOUR PERSONALITY NUMBER

Your Personality number is calculated from the day in the month on which you were born. For example, if you were born on the 23rd of the month, your Personality Number is a 23/5 (2 + 3 = 5). Each of the numbers in this number has an influence over your life, but the single digit between 1 to 9 remains the most potent. Therefore, if you were born on the 23rd you may like to read up about that number 23/5, and then about the numbers 3 and 2, which will enable you to find out a little more information about these other numbers which are also influencing you.

BELOW Number 1 Personality; your self-confidence inspires you to put your unique qualities to good use in life.

Personality Numbers 1–31

1 Number 1 is the basis of everything; every number contains a 1 within it, so you may feel really special and unique! Perhaps this means that you like to be different, show off a little about who you are, or dress in an individual way so that people notice you. You travel through life with a strong sense of identity. You may also be focused, ambitious, and wilful.

2 Number 2 highlights your feminine energies: creative, intuitive, nurturing, caring, and warm. You may also be cautious, vulnerable, oversensitive, and you may be fearful of relating to people. Occasionally you may be confrontational or touchy. This number represents the measurer, so you may like to weigh up the pros and cons of life. Decision-making, particularly where important issues are concerned, may also be challenging. Perhaps you may refuse to listen to reason.

3 At times you may portray a still calmness, and at other times you may not appear to draw a breath as you talk 20 to the dozen! While generally being outgoing, freedom-loving, and expressive, you can also withdraw into your mind. Subjects such as philosophy, mysticism, politics, and religion may appeal to you. You have a wonderful sense of humor but can be frivolous or superficial.

4 You may be passionate, dynamic, and creative, and also have a very practical side. Security may be an issue for you, and you can also be overmaterialistic at times. Loyalty may be very important, and you may place great emphasis on maintaining long-term friendships. You can sometimes be unreliable and disorganized, and you may need boundaries, structure, and routine to help you survive.

5 This number highlights movement, and you may enjoy dancing and traveling and need constant change to keep your mind stimulated. Perhaps you are changeable and restless sometimes. Life fascinates you, and although you can be adventurous, you may also be addicted to searching for the spark in everyday life. Perceptive and clever, you like to know the facts about life, but you can also be sceptical sometimes. You love being verbal, and your vivaciousness lights up people's lives.

ABOVE Personality Number 4; loyalty and friendship are very important.

LEFT Typically, a person with a Personality Number 3 could be most expressive when musing about the mystical elements in life.

RIGHT Personality Number 6; people may consider you the life and soul of the party.

6 You are a sociable "people" person and you often enjoy having others around you. Loving, charitable, generous, and demonstrative, you like physical affection and seek beauty in life. Sometimes you go around wearing rose-tinted spectacles, and although you may seem angelic, you can be jealous, sarcastic, resentful, and even revengeful. Family duties may be an issue here, as you seek to find wholeness within yourself and in your life. Sensual and instinctual, you enjoy the good things in life.

7 You may create magic in your life, as you are a powerful materializer who can apply a positive mind to help manifest your ideas. When you are focusing on negative thoughts you can likewise be destructive at times, for example, the car breaks down because you intensely think you don't want to go to work! You are sensitive and intuitive, and can also be overimaginative and impatient with life. Perhaps you are withdrawn, or cut off from your feelings as you try to protect yourself from being hurt by situations in life.

BELOW With a Personality Number 7, you may be very protective toward others.

8 You may be charming and inspirational, and you like to be your own boss. You may be intellectual, serious, bold, and assertive, and you can be aggressive sometimes. You may be very organized, conscientious, and capable, but you can also be manipulative and controlling. Shrewd and sure of yourself, you may even be egotistic and hierarchical.

9 You can be fun-loving, extrovert, and creative, and liberal in your approach to life. You are learning to be adaptable to the different people and situations you find yourself in, but you can sometimes be overcritical of life. Perhaps you are too precise about how life should be, or how people should behave; you may be prudish, too. You generally like to educate yourself with useful information which can be passed on to others. Good manners could be a burning issue.

10/1 You may be a wise person who understands people from your all-round experience, because the number 10 contains all the numbers 1 to 9 within its sphere of knowledge. This may mean you can be cynical at times, full of your own self-importance, or even forceful when you think you know everything! You may also stand up for people's rights, and sometimes be a flag waver. Dynamic and energetic, you may be very creative and enjoy working toward your goals with definite purpose.

11/2 You may be intuitive, receptive, and a good listener, and also a natural healer. Finely tuned and full of nervous energy, you may be easily excitable and temperamental sometimes. You generally have high expectations, and are disappointed when life doesn't come up to scratch. You tend to be single-minded in your ambitions, therefore success and even recognition may come your way as you go for life 100 percent. Intense and sensitive, you may develop inertia, particularly when you fear failure or rejection.

12/3 You can be caring and considerate, warm and gentle, with a need to look after others. You can also be fussy about whom you allow into your life, and you can be protective at times. Perhaps you enjoy cooking, painting, or writing; you seek ways to express yourself. You may enjoy parties and socializing – perhaps you are the center of attention – but you also enjoy intellectual conversation. However, your thoughts can easily become scattered and so can you.

13/4 You may love to stay up and converse all night as you enjoy talking with your nearest and dearest, and are seldom lost for words. You may be very determined and have the power to persevere, even when you are facing challenges. Perhaps you fear monotony or humdrum situations, so you may look for a touch of drama to keep you going. Inner conflicts may arise, particularly when you feel confused about your direction; sometimes you listen to your instincts and at other times your logical mind guides you.

14/5 You may be introspective and enjoy wrapping yourself up in research, study, or situations that are absorbing or develop your mind. You may have lots of practical ideas to help people, and when you are around, things usually get done quickly and well. Your quick-thinking mind means that sometimes words pour out before you've given them a second thought, which can sometimes get you into deep water. However, you may also have a tendency to restrict yourself in life.

15/6 You are a pleasure-seeking person, sometimes to the exclusion of all else; you may make sure your cup is full before everybody else's. Perhaps you love giving pleasure to others, and sometimes you may be overgenerous since you feel this is your role in life, and in extremes you may become a martyr to your good deeds. At times you are able to step out of yourself and see the bigger picture in order to get a more rounded perspective on life. You are one of life's little helpers.

LEFT Personality Number 11/2; instead of dominating a conversation, learn to be receptive to other people's points of view.

15

BELOW Having your head in the clouds may lead to frustration as you may misread a situation and feel let down.

19

RIGHT With an 18/9 Personality, you could be brilliant at directing people.

16/7 Artistic and creative, you may appreciate beauty, but at times glamorize things because you prefer to avoid the sometimes harsh realities of life. You may also be a perfectionist and go over and over things – at times at an almost obsessive level – in order to attain perfection. Sometimes you may be detached and cool. At other times you may be warm, nurturing, and caring, with a heart full of love and show affection to those around you.

17/8 You may be a strong and independent person, and a natural leader who can bring out the best in people. You have the ability to instigate things and motivate people, sometimes even without trying. You may like to do things your own way and you can be stubborn and rigid at times. Trusting yourself and others may be an issue. You may be impatient and sometimes isolate yourself from life. You have the ability to pay fine attention to detail, but you can be too fussy or picky at times.

BELOW Discover positive ways of working with perfectionism – a characteristic of the 16/7 Personality.

18/9 You may enjoy power through leadership, but sometimes this can take control of your life as you think the world stops and begins with you! You need to learn humility and how to direct your energy in a selfless way to serve others. You may even be dic-

RIGHT With an 18/9 Personality, you could be brilliant at directing people.

tatorial at times, but you may also like being told what to do, particularly when you feel directionless. Religion or politics may play a part in your life, and expressing yourself through art or writing may be preferable. You have a discriminating mind and like to work with the known facts rather than fiction.

19/10/1 You have strong passions and beliefs and will fight to the end in order to preserve them, but you can sometimes be patronizing to others. People may therefore look to you for leadership. You may at other times seek approval, particularly from your peers, and humiliation may be one of your deepest fears. You may be quite laid-back and relaxed about life, sometimes even too care-free, letting issues or situations go instead of dealing with them head on. Perhaps this is because you fear losing your sometimes fiery temper or losing the battle (if it is a case of opinions). You may enjoy social contact, particularly with those at the top of the tree.

20/2 You are a mediator and can stand in the middle of a situation and be an anchor for both sides; perhaps you also do this to keep the peace, because you feel uncomfortable with disharmony. Gentle and placid, you may sometimes be ambiguous so as to avoid offending anyone in your vicinity. You can be caring, and considerate. However, sometimes you may neglect to take good care of yourself. Moody and emotional, you have at times the ability to make your presence felt. You enjoy sharing with people too.

21/3 You generally have a huge amount of energy and enthusiasm to give to life, but occasionally you can overdo things as you try to take on too many tasks at once. This scattering of energies means that you can easily feel drained or exhausted; perhaps you can learn to list your priorities or to refocus on the important issues of the day. Lively and witty, you make a good host as you are also happy-go-lucky. Family issues, as well as freedom and self-expression, may be particularly important to you.

22/4 You are generally hard working and persevere to accomplish your goals in a step-by-step manner. You may feel insecure at times, and therefore like to build strong foundations to support you throughout your life; for example, a steady job, a long term relationship, and solid friendships. Openness and honesty may be important issues. You are learning to relate to life and to people through your emotions, although the depth of your feelings may also be challenging at times. You are loving, warm, and affectionate, and this shows through in your general view of people, and you also take a practical approach towards life and the way you live it.

23/5 You enjoy living your life to the full because it fascinates you; there is so much to see, do, and learn – and you try to fit it all in. You are romantic, with a strong, vivid imagination, and you are also playful and full of the joys of nature. Paradoxically, you may at times find that you are only interested in the facts and figures of life and get too caught up in how everything works. You may possess a brilliant brain, a creative streak of genius, or be incredibly laid-back about life, but, whatever the case, the sun still shines for you!

24/6 You have a very strong sense of responsibility, particularly towards family, and you may feel the need to provide. You may be time-conscious and aware of how much needs to be done in a day. You may be very musical, which can sometimes help to calm and soothe your stresses away. When duty calls, you generally deliver, but you may bear grudges if people seem to block the way of your own desires. You are learning to give with an open heart, and learning to love yourself and others.

BELOW Being a provider (24/6), you may enjoy listening to music to ease the pressures of an active day.

RIGHT Number 25/7; make the most out of life through your level-headed optimism and straight-talking.

25/7 Sensitive and spiritual, you can be like a delicate rose petal tentatively opening under the rays of the sun. You can be withdrawn and isolated at times, appearing detached and aloof; you may even become a hermit as you shelter yourself from life. You might need and enjoy privacy, too. Sometimes you appear naive, but you have a sharp mind and are fully able to communicate what you need. Appreciation may be an issue, and you are learning to take each day as it comes.

26/8 You may find yourself looking after and caring for people, particularly children, because you have such a warm, loving, and caring nature. Sometimes you may give too much and need to learn to say no; for example, when people come knocking on your door for the upteenth time or are demanding all of your attention and time. You may be prone to emotional outbursts because of your acute sensitivity, and you may sometimes throw tantrums as you disperse blocked energy. You often prefer to be the top of the class or the best, and you may be authoritarian. Indeed you can feel deflated or hurt when others shine around you, and you might be prone to jealousy.

RIGHT Personality Number 26/8; discover new ways to channel your energies when you feel emotionally drained.

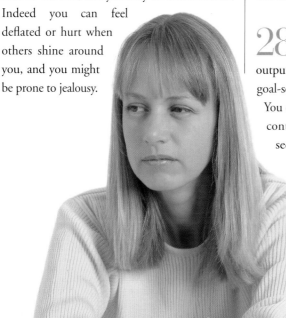

27/9 You could cope well in a leadership role, and people may regard you as a parent figure. You appear to be able to stay in control of a sinking ship and have a commanding aura about you. You tend to get straight to the point and people usually know exactly where they stand with you. Intellectual, bright, open to life, you can also be extremely passionate, but learning to relax and connect with your inner self may be an issue. A natural teacher, if only by the example you set. You are one of life's givers.

28/10/1 You may be an ambitious person whose creative output leaves others in the shade at times, and goal-setting might have been invented by you. You can also be compulsive, as your goals take control of you at times. Money might play second fiddle to your creative needs and your need to materialize your ideas and act on these impulses. You may be strongly independent and enjoy working things out for yourself. However, sometimes you dissolve into emotion, and you may at these times lose your motivation for life.

29/11/2 You have an ability to inspire others with your creativity and sensitivity toward life. You may be highly strung and thrive off your nervous energy, but your mood swings can at times push others away. You are driven with a passion for life and goal-setting is often serious business, but your fear of failure could hold you back. At other times you keep on trying anyway. You enjoy peace and harmony, although life in the fast lane means that you may need to work hard to achieve this.

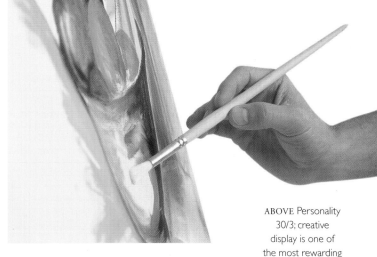

ABOVE Personality 30/3; creative display is one of the most rewarding outlets for self-expression.

30/3 You are blessed with abundant creativity and, whether you express yourself verbally or with your hands, this energy seems to flow effortlessly! Sometimes you go into chaos and confusion, but then you may delve into your own inner wisdom to find a resolve, which can be extremely productive. You can be cynical and pessimistic about life at times, but your happy nature eventually shines through. You may sail through life like it is one big party, or manage not to take life's little challenges too seriously.

31/4 You are earthy and sensual and may enjoy responsibilities as much as having a good laugh. Perhaps you stand out from the crowd or feel extra-special. You may also feel that you have a special task to carry out to benefit the world in some way. You are generally very focused and keep your mind on your chosen quest; however, the reverse of this is that you may seem blinkered and can be too rigid in your view of life at times. Popular, you may possess an air of mystery, although you have the ability to instantly put people at ease and can make people laugh.

31

LEFT Number 31/4; with the ambition and drive of a dedicated athlete, you look to achieve a single goal with steely determination.

LIFE PATH NUMBERS

★ ★ ★ ★ ★ ★ ★ ★ ★ ★ ★ ★ ★ ★ ★ ★ ★

YOUR LIFE PATH or Life Purpose Number highlights your purpose within the bigger picture or greater plan of life. It can also be described as your direction in life, or the path you take. Sometimes people regard their Life Path with awe, but in effect it is very simple. The emphasis you place upon your goals or direction makes it seem larger than life.

Particularly when you are young, you are governed by your Personality wants and desires. As you get older you generally start to look around to see what is going on in the outside world. Life is asking you to be yourself and to learn by the experiences that come your way. Some people work strongly with their Life Path Numbers from an early age, while others may not be aware of their application until middle age or even later.

Your Life Path Number is calculated by adding up all the numbers in your date of birth. If you were born on July 29 1981, then look at the table above right.

Consult your Life Path Number here to find what it highlights. You may also like to look up the digits proceeding this number 1 in the calculation, which in the above example are the numbers 5, to find out other influences over your Life Path, but the single numeral between 1 and 9 always has the most important influence on you.

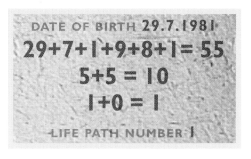

DATE OF BIRTH 29.7.1981
$$29+7+1+9+8+1 = 55$$
$$5+5 = 10$$
$$1+0 = 1$$
LIFE PATH NUMBER 1

Life Path 1

With a 1 as your Life Path Number, you are working toward individualization so that you can learn to be yourself. Once you are comfortable with yourself, you can make an impact with your leadership and focus in life, which concentrates not on yourself but on collective or group ideas and goals that need to be accomplished. You are confident to speak your mind and are unafraid of confronting even the biggest challenges in life. Sometimes you may be dictatorial and resort to using power for yourself.

ABOVE Your Life Path Number helps to guide you toward achieving your aspirations.

LEFT Single-minded and resourceful – qualities influenced by the Number 1, and shared by many world sports personalities.

many countries in the world and bring people together on issues. Self-expression may sometimes be an issue too.

LEFT Diplomacy is synonymous with balancing people's needs.

Life Path 4

You may feel comfortable within yourself, and this feeling of ease may enable you to take on enormous amounts of responsibility for others. Perhaps you feel the need of the collective group as a strong pull at times, and your practical streak means that you may like to help others to survive. Perhaps you also encourage people to take responsibility for themselves too, instead of you taking responsibility for them. Sometimes you may feel trapped within the boundaries or the confines of certain responsibilities, but when you see practical results from your efforts, then it may help you to carry on.

BELOW Perhaps a qualified medical professional, you thrive on responsibility and can offer people reassurance.

Life Path 2

You are sensitive and aware of the fine balancing act in life, and you like to see co-operation between people, particularly in delicate world situations. You may be diplomatic and tolerant and a fine negotiator, especially on behalf of others. You may also be demanding and take sides, and you feel you can only win or lose in any situation. This creates an imbalance within yourself and a lack of peace, as you may feel at war with others. You are learning to understand the meaning of love and compassion for the group.

Life Path 3

Creativity is an outer expression of the inner world of soul and spirit, and you may be highly active in expressing this to the world. You have the ability to uplift others through your joy of living. Communicating through creativity may open doors to allow others to connect with themselves. For example, a speech by an important politician can be heard simultaneously in

Life Path 5

Change is inevitable and with this Life Path 5 Number in your chart, you are learning to keep communicating, for the collective group, when changes occur. For example, if you continue to communicate in difficult situations within your family group then it may help everyone around you. Sometimes you may jump to conclusions and overreact, or you may be very changeable in addressing people around you. Clarity in your communication can help yourself and others.

Life Path 6

Service is highlighted here and this means doing what is best for the whole group and not simply yourself. Service can mean doing simple things, like bringing a beautiful bunch of flowers home for your whole family, or baking a sumptuous cake for your colleagues, brightening everyone's day. Sometimes service means doing things you don't always want to do but which are truly needed, and often when you recognize the group's needs you may feel compelled to surrender. Service comes out of true love of goodness, but you may also sometimes try to help others in order to make yourself feel good.

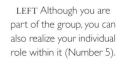

LEFT Life Path 8: you like guiding others, particularly in business, and you enjoy collective success.

Life Path 7

Your powers of intuition, along with positive thoughts and actions, can guide you to manifest others' needs. You are learning to trust your intuition and to believe in yourself, and you may find that when you do so you are guided in the best possible way for all concerned. You are often able to see the truth in a given situation, even when others are struggling; you are also being challenged to trust your own truth (rather than someone else's).

Life Path 8

Your Life Path is guiding you to find strength for the collective, particularly during challenging times. You may lead others with a strong direction and a powerful will, driving everyone forward with their lives, and carving a positive way forward. Your strength may seem overpowering to others sometimes, and you may take your leading role too seriously. Perhaps you feel disempowered by other strong leaders within your group, and sometimes you may need to surrender to the stronger power, which comes from within you.

Life Path 9

With a Life Path Number 9 you may change colors with the wind and be so adaptable that you fit into people's lives without them even noticing you around. This is how you serve others: by getting your own needs out of the way and by being adaptable to others' needs and to every situation that you experience in life. You are in this way working toward selflessness, as you dissolve into the collective need.

BELOW With Life Path 9, you unthinkingly set your own needs aside in order to help others.

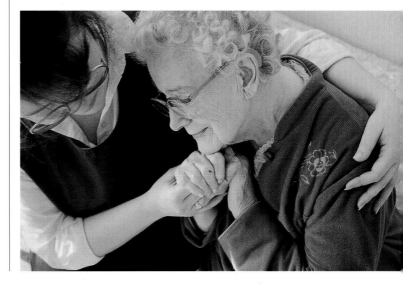

SOUL NUMBERS

★ ★ ★ ★ ★ ★ ★ ★ ★ ★ ★ ★ ★ ★ ★ ★ ★

Y OUR SOUL NUMBER highlights some of the deeper elements within your chart and your life. Your soul is the essence of you that travels on after your physical body dies, and it belongs to a single group soul in the way that on earth you are part of the human family. Deep down inside yourself, you are able to contact your soul. Great inventors, mathematicians, humanitarians, and world leaders use this inner guidance to guide them with their lives, though they may make conscious decisions and take actions influenced by their Personality Number too.

Your Soul Number interacts with your whole chart, particularly with your Life Path Number, which also contains elements of soul within it. Your Personality and your Life Path Numbers may struggle with each other (one can be selfish and the other might look at the whole group's needs). This may well intensify when the presence from your Soul Number is felt strongly in your life by you.

To calculate your Soul Number you simply add up all the vowels in the full name on your birth certificate by translating each letter into a number from the alphabet box here. If you do not have a birth certificate, use the first full names by which you were first known, which were given to you at birth and therefore have a strong connection with your life and the lessons you need to learn.

As an example, the name "William Michael Davenport" is used:

RIGHT Your Soul Number connects you more closely to your inner self.

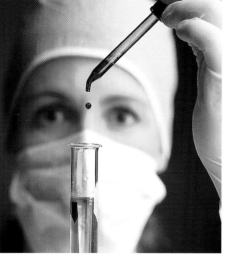

ABOVE Scientific breakthroughs have not only enabled the world to constantly evolve, they have taught individuals the wisdom of learning through experience.

William Michael Davenport			
9 9 1 9 15 1 5 6			
A	J	S	1
B	K	T	2
C	L	U	3
D	M	V	4
E	N	W	5
F	O	X	6
G	P	Y	7
H	Q	Z	8
I	R		9

$$9+9+1+9+1+5+$$
$$1+5+6=46$$

William Michael Davenport

$$4+6=10 \quad 1+0=1$$

SOUL NUMBER 1

Soul Number 1

Your soul is guiding you toward new frontiers and to break old ground as you go through life, and sometimes to tread on paths which have been untouched by mankind. You may be able to build things easily with your pioneering spirit. For example, you could design a new piece of machinery that others can use as a building block in many different areas of commerce. At times your life may seem to fall apart while you go through the process of inner self-discovery or of rebuilding your life for yourself and others in some way.

Soul Number 2

This Soul Number highlights the need to develop wisdom and compassion on your journey through life. Perhaps you find that you can apply this easily at times, while maintaining a non-partial view to situations or people. Wisdom is gained by experience and through learning about life first-hand, and therefore every experience in life is knowledge that can shine through your soul to help others. Life is simple and sometimes you may make it more complicated by clouding it with your emotions so that you are unable to see the wisdom of what life is teaching you.

Soul Number 3

This Soul Number is guiding you toward beingness and an acceptance of life as it is. Even if you only experience this a few times in life you can recognize that this is your soul shining through. This means accepting yourself too, though the depths of your shadow side may sometimes make this challenging. Of course, you are human, and few people can accept life fully, but learning to go with the flow and accepting life's lessons mean that you are listening to your soul.

Soul Number 4

With a Soul Number 4 you are being guided toward bringing harmony into the lives of yourself and others, particularly on the physical level. Indeed, you may be a practical guide, and you are also learning to be realistic about life, too. Keeping your feet on the ground may require discipline, but your soul is always there to guide you to find new ways to reside comfortably in the physical world. You are also learning to build solid foundations for yourself and others, so that you can remain strong in any situation.

LEFT Soul Number 2; you are guided to help others in a foreign country.

29

ABOVE Evelyn de Morgan's romantic painting entitled *The Passing of the Soul* is a highly-charged depiction of a soul about to depart from the mortal earth.

Soul Number 5 *x me*

Your Soul Number is guiding you toward communication with your inner self so that you can then transmit messages from your soul to the outside world. Sometimes these may be profound as they stimulate others' minds, and at times you may be surprised by what you convey to the world. At other times you may glamorize the words you speak, which may be your Personality talking rather than your soul, even though sometimes this may seem the only way to make people listen to what you have to say. Communication can also take place on different levels and you may express this soul energy in other ways; for example, by using the power of telepathy.

Soul Number 6

Your Soul Number is guiding you to learn to live life by experiencing it for what it is. Love of the soul in its purest form is unconditional, but when translated into human form, becomes lost in attachments to physical desires. This is because you love the outer garment or Personality too much in its seeming perfection. The soul follows its own path, and it can be difficult for you to change or alter this. When you have unlovable thoughts, this may inevitably be as the result of conflict between your personality's wants and desires and the needs of your soul. You are human, and everyone makes mistakes, but your soul is teaching you to love humanity for better or for worse.

Soul Number 7

The number 7 is linked with the emotions and your soul is teaching you to develop a sensitivity toward life. This does not mean becoming so fragile that you cannot function in the everyday world, but becoming sensitive to the needs of others and to anticipate their needs. Sensitivity is a strength when you put it to good use, but you can become lost in your own emotions at times. Your Soul Number is highlighting introspection as a way home on the journey to your soul, but by developing your own self-awareness your soul can teach others how to contact their spirituality and find their inner connection too.

Soul Number 8

With an 8 as a guiding Soul Number, pure spirituality may drive you on with your life in order to serve yourself and others. People may see in you the qualities of stubbornness and single-mindedness toward your own ambitions, but these goals may be to help others too. You may feel your soul as a force that you find difficult to resist as it guides you to certain actions in your life, but most of the time you may not question your inner direction since it is so strong. You may like to think you are in control of your life, but at the end of the day nature always has the last say.

Soul Number 9

Humor is one of the best teachers and your soul is bringing forth this quality in abundance; you are able to inspire others with this gift. Sometimes you feel pure joy as you express this soul energy out into the world. Your soul is also teaching you humility, and to take life in your stride as you learn to accept others and not judge them too harshly. This Soul Number can also teach you to have faith in life, and to believe in the soul or inner life as much as you believe in the power of outer everyday life. You may also be learning to liberate yourself from feelings of self-importance that you may experience.

LEFT Soul Number 8: you can be stubborn and willful, but these qualities can be used to help others.

ABOVE Number 9: being able to make people laugh is a gift.

LEFT Soul Number 7: your natural sensitivity to others sometimes serves as a sanctuary for introspection.

CHILDHOOD NUMBERS

★ ★ ★ ★ ★ ★ ★ ★ ★ ★ ★ ★ ★ ★ ★ ★ ★

WITH NUMEROLOGY numbers can influence you in different ways at different ages. When you are a child you are generally much more open and adaptable to life, so the way you choose to utilize these energies may change from day to day. Indeed, only in teenage years do children begin to develop a real sense of their own identity. The types of experiences children may have and the types of situations that may weave around them are highlighted in the Childhood Number. However the "inner child" is always within you; memories and patterns that were set in your early years stay with you, and therefore this number is relevant to everyone throughout life.

The Childhood Number also highlights energy carried with you from the past – particularly your previous lifetime – and therefore you may find some childhood issues particularly significant as you carry them through into your adult life.

Your Childhood Number is found by adding up all the consonants in your full name on your birth certificate (or in the full names by which you were first known). You can translate each letter into a number from the alphabet box here. For example:

BELOW A special one-to-one relationship with parents can help a child feel secure in the world.

| William Michael Davenport | | | |
5 33 4 4 38	34 4	57 92	
A	J	S	1
B	K	T	2
C	L	U	3
D	M	V	4
E	N	W	5
F	O	X	6
G	P	Y	7
H	Q	Z	8
I	R		9

5+3+3+4+4+3+8+3
+4+4+5+7+9+2=64,
6+4=10, 1+0=1
CHILDHOOD NUMBER 1

32

rather cautious and fearful of situations, and perhaps you were rather shy and quiet.

LEFT As a child, you may have had an insatiable appetite for reading.

Childhood Number 3

Life as a child may have been full of play, or rather you made everything, including school work, seem like fun. Perhaps this was because you liked to laugh at life (and pull faces at people), and this may well have landed you in trouble with your parents and teachers at times. Mischievous and naughty, you could also be a little angel at times, and did your homework without being asked and generally liked to help people. You may have been an active child at sport and play, sometimes leaving a trail of untidiness. You were likely to have enjoyed quiet times reading and studying.

Childhood Number 1

With a 1 in childhood, you may have been self-centered and thought that the earth revolved around you; perhaps you were an only child or made to feel extra-special by doting adults. Sometimes you may have felt left out or that you didn't fit into your home, school, or social situations. Perhaps you liked to be alone and needed to be beckoned out into the world from your room or your own inner world. You may have been very independent and enjoyed doing things on your own.

Childhood Number 2

You may have been a very sensitive child, or one who cried easily; sometimes this may have been because you were unable to relate to people, or because you felt and expressed the pain of those close to you. You may have been very moody, too. But you may have possessed a kind heart and were always the first to share your candies with your friends and family. You may have enjoyed caring for pets or dolls or for other brothers and sisters who were around. At times, though, you could be

LEFT Open-hearted as a youngster, your close affinity with your siblings may have helped you to harness your outer shyness.

Childhood Number 4

You may have been a conscientious child who applied yourself to life thoroughly, whether baking cakes or working on a school project. Perhaps you experienced a certain amount of discipline in your home life, helping you to stay focused, or perhaps you were full of determination. However, you may have experienced few boundaries and therefore felt insecure at times, or felt like you were given no direction. Art and music may have lifted your spirits and helped you to relax and enjoy your life more.

Childhood Number 5

In your childhood you may have been a popular person with plenty of choice about your friends. However, you may have been very changeable and played hot and cold about whom you wanted around you, as you were probably restless at times. Perhaps you often left books unread and projects incomplete, including your homework, and made excuses why you couldn't finish what you started. You may have needed plenty of stimulation because of your active mind, and therefore you may have appeared demanding sometimes.

Childhood Number 6

You were probably happy to nestle with your family and friends, and enjoyed physical affection, or seemed to need extra amounts of love and affection as a child. At times, though, you may have felt emotionally smothered by too much mothering, while at other times you may yourself have been demanding of others both emotionally and physically. Perhaps you wallowed in emotion in order to get some attention, or even whined and complained about your lot in life. You may also have relished having lots of children and people around you. Possibly you had a comfort-providing and contented childhood.

$$1 \times 2 = 2$$
$$2 \times 2 = 4$$
$$3 \times 2 = 6$$
$$4 \times 2 =$$

Childhood Number 7

In your childhood you may have been happy to sit staring into space for hours, drifting off into the world of your own imagination. You may have been very spiritual, intuitively expressing things with great clarity to those around you. You may have been quite a thinker, who liked solitude, but you could also feel isolated from the general activities of life. Sometimes you may have found entertaining yourself a challenge, and friends with strong characters who could help bring you out were likely to be popular with you. You were probably self-aware when you were a child, and may even have been precocious at times.

Childhood Number 8

Multi-talented as a child, you may also have enjoyed showing off those talents to whoever was around. You may have been quite precocious and delighted in being the center of attention – making sure everyone was looking at you. Smart and bold, you probably had problems solved in your head before they even seemed to arise and generally you liked to be one step ahead. You may have also been precise, possibly pernickerty, particularly in the way that you dressed, and even as a child you may have wanted to always look your very best. Sometimes you may have been trying or testing to your family or friends because of your insecurity, and you may have been bossy and uncontrollable. However, you probably had some ability to rein yourself in.

Childhood Number 9

As a child you may have loved to learn about life from books, from school, and from the experiences of others around you, especially your family. Perhaps at times it seemed like you could not learn fast enough, as you always wanted to find out more. You may also have come across as a "goody two shoes," always on your best behavior or at the top of the class. Paradoxically, this desire for knowledge may have meant that you possessed a strong rebellious streak, enabling you to find out about life in ways certainly not acceptable to the adults around you. Perhaps you had judgemental parents, and you may have been overly critical or judgemental about yourself.

LEFT Number 8 is quick and bright, and can solve problems swiftly.

LEFT Number 9; a keen aptitude for learning, you may have wanted to tarnish your clean image with rebellious behavior.

KARMA AND KARMA NUMBERS

KARMA IS SUCH a significant subject that it is helpful to learn more about how it relates to numerology. Understanding karma can help you to make the most of your life. Each number in your personal numerology chart highlights some form of karma, particularly your Karma Number and your Soul Number. These numbers point to your previous lifetimes and help establish karma you may have been working through before.

ABOVE Karma educates you about responsibility. It can teach you much more than any book.

WHAT IS KARMA?

Karma is the law of cause and effect: what you give out, you get back. Karma influences everyone and everything on this planet and in the universe. It is something by which all people live, even if they do not realize it. For example, have you ever parked your car in a space belonging to someone else at work, but later that day gone home to find somebody has parked his or her car in your space there? This is karma in operation!

All karma is essentially good, because it is teaching you more about the lessons you need to learn in life. It also highlights the need to make decisions and take responsibility for your own choices, thoughts, and actions. Indeed, negative karma sometimes can be transformed into positive karma by simple awareness or recognition of what life is teaching you, or by a resolve to let negative patterns go and to approach life in a positive way or with a different attitude next time round.

You may think that karma means that by being good you always attract good things to you, but negative karma from the past may catch up with you at the precise moment you are being a little angel. Even though you may

RIGHT No point crying over spilt milk, learn your lessons and then move on.

have long since forgotten what you did, the past always catches up with you. Everyone learns different lessons at different times of their evolution. Such is life.

COLLECTIVE KARMA

Although it may seem that your own personal karma is of the greatest significance to you, the collective karma – the karma from the groups to which you belong, including the whole of humanity – actually has the most influence over your life. Indeed, as you individually get your own just deserts from the past, then the group does so collectively, too. Wherever you are in the world you are reaping collective karma from the past.

Karma can also be seen working its way out through your family collective or group, which in numerology is highlighted in your family name or surname.

TYPES OF KARMA

Karma may occur at different levels, or in many different areas at once. Each realm influences the others, since mind, body, and spirit are inextricably linked as one.

Physical: If you have the numbers 4 or 5 in your chart as a Karma Number, you may be very aware of your physical body, and you may pay particular attention to how things influence you practically or physically.

Emotional: If you have the number 2, 3, or 6 as your Karma Number, then you may be acutely aware of your feelings and your emotional desires. Karma may be particularly expressed or felt much more intensely on the emotional level of your body.

Mental: If you have the numbers 1 or 8 as your Karma Number, then you may be pre-occupied with mental thought-forms and how people interact and create karma from the level of mind. Positive thoughts help create positive karma, and vice versa.

Spiritual: If you have the numbers 7 or 9 as your Karma Number, then you may be blessed with awareness of spiritual karma, and you may feel the collective karma of humanity strongly, too. Spirituality doesn't reward you or punish you, but it can connect you with the wisdom contained within each karmic lesson.

CREATING YOUR FUTURE

You are contributing toward the creation of your future every moment of the day, individually and collectively. Numerology can help you to identify your karmic trends and highlights collective karma that needs to be brought into the light in order to be released and help create a brighter future.

Your Karma Number highlights qualities and gifts that you have developed in the past. Sometimes it is referred to as your Wisdom Number because it is the sum total of all your experiences to date. Like all the other numbers in your chart, your Karma Number contains strengths and challenges, but you may find that the gifts associated with this number are strong. Your Karma Number contains elements of soul, as it encompasses soul memories of all that has gone before.

You do not need to believe in past lives to be influenced by this number. You may prefer to regard it as being determined by all your experiences in this life. However, issues that arise from the influence of this number may spark off memories from the past. Everybody also has a collective or group memory from the past, so certain things may be recalled because they are so deeply ingrained in the world subconscious memory bank.

Your Karma Number is the fourth most important number in your chart – after your Personality, Life Path and your Soul Number – these numbers all interact to give your life the shape that it has. All these energies blend together to form the unique you.

LEFT You may be particularly aware of how karma influences you physically, e.g. if you overdo the exercise you may really ache the next day but also feel the positive mental benefits.

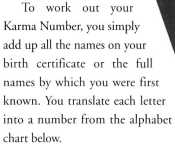

RIGHT Your Karma Number is derived from all the names by which you were first known.

To work out your Karma Number, you simply add up all the names on your birth certificate or the full names by which you were first known. You translate each letter into a number from the alphabet chart below.

William Michael Davenport
5933914 4938153 414557892

A	J	S	1
B	K	T	2
C	L	U	3
D	M	V	4
E	N	W	5
F	O	X	6
G	P	Y	7
H	Q	Z	8
I	R	Z	9

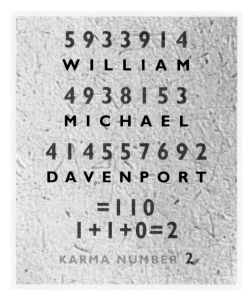

5933914
W I L L I A M
4938153
M I C H A E L
414557692
D A V E N P O R T
= 110
1 + 1 + 0 = 2
KARMA NUMBER 2

Karma Number 1
One of your gifts for this lifetime is the ability to see a clear direction ahead. You may be very good at showing people the way and, like a shepherd, enjoy leading your flock to safety. This is because you have a strong will guiding you forward, even though at times you feel blindly led. Sometimes you may not want this role; when others have a real need for a leader, you are likely to assume the role automatically.

Karma Number 2
In the past you may have been a peacemaker or a decision-maker for those around you. As this is one of your gifts, you may today enjoy decision-making, but if you feel that your decisions can cause disharmony, then you may resist making choices. Wisdom is the ability to make decisions based upon your experiences. Therefore every decision you make today, is contributing toward this skill.

Karma Number 3
In the past you may have been a mystic whose understanding of the inner life was very potent, so the gift of inner knowledge is one of your gifts today. Knowledge can come from the experiences of all your past lives. Sometimes you may express your knowledge through communication, art, music, literature, or working with your hands, because the 3 energy is very creative.

Karma Number 4
Your gift is your ability to remain calm in a storm and keep your feet firmly on the ground, even when it is crumbling beneath you. In the past you may have been a dependable rock to

others because you were willing to take responsibility for yourself, which is a gift. However, you could at times want others to shoulder your responsibilities.

Karma Number 5

With a scientific or logical mind, in the past you may have enjoyed and been gifted at working out the facts and the figures of everyday life. You may have been able to communicate your view of reality to those around you or the wider world. Today you may be sceptical about life, or you may use your factual mind to help you handle everyday life.

Karma Number 6

You may have applied your love for humanity and your inner wisdom to help people with their lives in the past. Sometimes you may have found that you gave too much and tired yourself out, particularly emotionally, even if you enjoyed every moment. A capacity to see the whole picture may be one of your gifts.

Karma Number 7

In the past you may have been someone who gave spiritual guidance to your community or to those around you; perhaps you did this in the field of commerce, the arts, religion, or politics. You may have been guided by your very strong intuition, which was perhaps one of your gifts.

Karma Number 8

In the past you may have been strongly influenced by the effects of karma, and experienced powerful learning. Karma is actually teaching you about taking responsibility for your thoughts and your actions, which may be your gift from the past. By teaching responsibility it can help you to move forward in your life in a much more positive way.

ABOVE Karma Number 3; you may possess a special gift for music.

Karma Number 9

In the past you may have possessed an open mind, which made you popular with people. Today you may be a very opinionated person, eager to win people over to your own viewpoint. Paradoxically you may also be covert, expressing your beliefs in secret, perhaps fearful that your views will meet the disapproval of others. Perhaps your gift from the past is your countless ability to remain flexible about life.

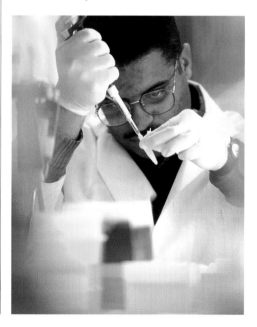

FAR LEFT Karma Number 1; you may be an elected leader.

LEFT Karma Number 5; you may have a gifted mind.

THE SIGNIFICANCE OF EACH OF YOUR NAMES

* * * * * * * * * * * * * * * *

YOUR DATE OF birth is extremely important and accounts for much of your make-up in terms of the kinds of experiences you may have, your strengths, your challenges, and your potential in life. But your names are also significant because overall they give you additional influences from your soul, from your childhood, and from your past experiences.

Each of your individual Name Numbers is also important, taking different roles in influencing your life, each with their own vibration of energy. Your names are ways by which people identify you and are important because they are the way you are introduced when first meeting people. Have you ever thought "That's a nice name" or "I like that person" when you first meet them? This grows out of their energy, and their names and their dates of birth carry these qualities.

In numerology your first name highlights some of your goals in life, but it can also give you indications of energies that you have been working with in the past. These goals are simple, but you may find many different ways of working toward these goals. Your middle names are there to support you with the lessons you need to learn from your first name, and in working on your life goals. Finally, your Family Name highlights issues that your family group is working on collectively and can show you where some of your hereditary gifts, strengths, and challenges emerge from to have an influence.

Each individual Name Number contributes toward your identity. With twins who have the same date of birth these energies will certainly highlight differences that make each of them

unique. Understanding more about your names is not only fun but essential, as self-awareness can help you to develop your full potential.

To work out your individual Name Numbers simply add up each name by translating each letter into numbers from the alphabet.

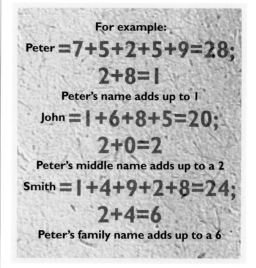

For example:
Peter = 7+5+2+5+9=28; 2+8=1
Peter's name adds up to 1
John = 1+6+8+5=20; 2+0=2
Peter's middle name adds up to a 2
Smith = 1+4+9+2+8=24; 2+4=6
Peter's family name adds up to a 6

ABOVE First Name Number 5; you may empathise with many of the great composers, past and present.

RIGHT You may identify with the beauty of a natural landscape if your First Name Number is 6, as it reflects simplicity in its perfection.

Name Number Chart

A	J	S	1
B	K	T	2
C	L	U	3
D	M	V	4
E	N	W	5
F	O	X	6
G	P	Y	7
H	Q	Z	8
I	R		9

First Name

1 One of your goals is to work toward your independence and to be able to function on your own in the everyday world and rely on yourself.

2 One of your goals is to learn to co-operate with people and with life so that you can accomplish win-win situations, and so that you can feel at one with life.

3 To learn to think and act thoughtfully is one of your goals, so that you do not amble into situations in life, but actively focus on what you need to do.

4 One of your goals is to learn to materialize your own physical needs, so that you can survive in the material world by taking responsibility for yourself.

5 Connection to others through self-expression is one of the goals you are working toward, so that you can communicate from your soul.

6 One of your goals is to learn to appreciate beauty, and to appreciate the beauty in imperfection, because life is always in a state of constant perfection (it is as it is).

7 One of your goals is to learn to live in the physical world by emersing yourself in the whole group (family, friends, community), instead of isolating yourself.

8 One of your goals is to learn to let go of the need to be in control, so that you can allow others to be themselves and do what they need to do, not try to force them to be how you want them to be.

9 Learning to allow yourself the freedom to be yourself is one of the goals you are working with, so that you set others free too.

BELOW If your First Name Number is 7, your goal may be to immerse yourself in a close network of friends and family as a means of gaining self-awareness.

LEFT Number 2; learning to resolve conflict with people through co-operation is a positive step for you.

Middle Name(s)

1 This 1 energy can support you by helping you to focus on life, and to remain steady in your focus so that you can head forward in the direction you choose.

2 A 2 energy can help to support you emotionally so that you can instinctively feel what needs to be said or done in any situation in life.

3 You can be supported by this 3 energy of activity so that it can help you to expand your horizon by expressing yourself in all areas of your life.

4 This 4 energy can help support you by teaching you to keep your feet on the ground so that you can be productive with the endeavors you undertake.

5 This 5 energy can support you by helping you to be aware of times when you need to communicate and times when it is good to keep quiet for the sake of all concerned.

6 This number 6 can help support you with its joyous outlook on life, and enable you also to spread your ray of sunshine to those around you.

7 This 7 energy can support you by helping you to see life as a wonderful journey of personal development, so that you can quickly learn those important lessons that you need to learn in life.

8 The energy of the number 8 can support you by bringing to your awareness the spiritual (or inner) and the material (or outer) elements in life so that you can learn to balance both.

9 This 9 energy can support you by encouraging you to let things go and let things flow, and give you faith that life is leading you in the direction where you need to go in order to grow.

5 With a 5 Family Name Number you may enjoy traveling in your mind or around the globe, and so you may be restless if you feel tied down or tied to each other for periods of time.

6 With a 6 as your Family Name Number, you may be learning to provide for each other as part of a whole group, and to learn to be responsible for the group's needs.

7 With a 7 Family Name Number, you are learning to trust each other and therefore you may feel betrayed if you find that someone has let you down.

8 With an 8 Family Name Number, you are learning to handle power in a positive way and to empower others within your everyday lives, but there may be power struggles at times.

9 You may be all learning about education with a 9 Family Name Number, but you may try to outshine each other by your polished encyclopedia of knowledge about life.

LEFT With a 4 Family Name Number, you are learning to relate to others physically.

BELOW Number 2; sharing emotional issues with your partner may help reinforce the relationship's foundations.

Family Name

1 With a 1 as your Family Name Number, you may be learning to be pioneers or leaders, but you may clash if you all want to take the lead at the same time.

2 A number 2 is influencing your Family Name, so you may be collectively learning to relate to each other through your feelings or your emotions, which may sometimes seem challenging.

3 With a 3 Family Name Number, you may be learning as a group to be creative and expressive with each other, but you may at times have a care-less attitude toward your contribution.

4 With a 4 Family Name Number, you may be learning to live together in harmony on the nitty-gritty physical level, which may create much personal growth on everyone's behalf.

CHANGING YOUR NAMES

* * * * * * * * * * * * * * * *

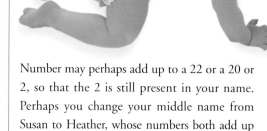

NUMEROLOGISTS ARE OFTEN asked to help people change their names because names emit tremendous power.

PERSONAL NAMES

RIGHT Children's names influence them all their lives.

You full names on your birth certificate, given to you by your parents or guardians, contain soul elements, childhood elements, and karmic elements. These names are very significant. If you are seeking to change your name, then you may on one level be trying to get away from lessons that you need to learn. For example, perhaps you are trying to escape your past identity or a challenging situation that you may have experienced. You may also want to change your name because you think you can earn more money or be more successful.

BELOW Adopting new names through remarriage gives you additional karma to work with.

The names you were given at birth and their numbers are always present in your chart, even if you do change your name, because these were energies given to you at birth; your make-up, in effect. By changing your name you are not only working toward fulfilling your original karma, but also taking on additional karma from the new names you are assuming.

It is often the case that if you do change to another name or names, then these, by synchronicity, contain similar energies or numbers to the ones given to you at your date of birth. For example, your Soul Number may be a 2 on your birth certificate. If you change your first name your Karma Number may perhaps add up to a 22 or a 20 or 2, so that the 2 is still present in your name. Perhaps you change your middle name from Susan to Heather, whose numbers both add up to a 2.

DERIVATIONS

Many people call themselves by shorter or longer versions of their own names, such as Kath for Katherine. You may also adapt names to suit your situation in life. For example, if your name is William, some people may call you Will, Wills, Bill, or Billy instead of your full name. Derivations are significant because they let you know what the person calling you by that name is projecting onto you or how they see you. Consider the name William. Perhaps William's parents call him by his first name, which adds up to a 7, because he is very sensitive; his personal trainer calls him Wills, which adds up to a 3 that highlights activity; his bank manager calls him Bill, an 8, which is a number associated with money; and his girlfriend calls him Billy, which adds up to a 6 that has qualities of affection and love.

What each person in your life calls you, gives you hidden information about your relationships. Sometimes you may not like your name derivation or pet name, either because you dislike some of the qualities it contains, or you do not feel comfortable with the type of relationship the name implies. For example, William may not like his bank manager calling him Billy, which his girlfriend calls him, because this feels too intimate, and so on.

MARRIAGE

Getting married is exciting for many people, and some women happily take on their partner's name, accepting the union of the energies which are being brought together. Of course, even in marriage the influence from the names on the birth certificate is still evident, but you are taking on additional energies to work with in your new married name. You may often find that you attract to you a partner whose Family Name, when mingled with yours, gives you numbers or qualities that are in your chart already and therefore need to be explored more thoroughly.

For example, Mary Amanda Cloves marries John Robinson.

```
Mary   =4197=21   2+1=3
Amanda =141541=16
       1+6=7
Cloves =336451=22
       2+2=4
Karma Total =3+7+4=14
       1+4=5
```

The total sum of all the numbers on her birth certificate add up to 5, which is her Karma Number.

When Mary marries she takes on her husband's name Robinson.

```
Mary   =4197=21   2+1=3
Amanda =141541=16
       1+6=7
Robinson =96295165=43
       4+3=5
```

ABOVE Adopting your spouse's name in marriage may highlight the qualities contained within your own chart.

Mary's whole name now adds up to an 8, which is Mary's Personality Number, as she was born on the 8th of the month, so by taking on her married name those energies (and her husband's) are helping her to learn more about the qualities already contained within her chart. Even if wives do not take on their husband's names at marriage, there are still lessons to teach each other, but they may be consciously keeping hold of their own identity by retaining the Family Name in their birth certificate. This may mean they still need to explore deeply their own family karma before moving onto other aspects of their chart with somebody else.

BUSINESS NAMES

Your identity in the field of business is very important and you may change your name to identify with the field or area where you work. For example, if you work as a public relations executive, then you may feel you need to have lots of 5s in your chart; and if you work as an accountant, then 4s and 8s may be the order of the day. However, as you were born with certain gifts, working with your existing names is always helpful.

Sometimes you can enhance your career or work by changing the initials or the names to bring out some of the qualities on your chart. For example, James Mark Johnson (55/1) may change his name to James M. Johnson (43/7) to enhance his career as a maths teacher, and so on.

BELOW Choosing a name for a business or project is really important; numerology helps you identify the best potential.

PERSONAL AND UNIVERSAL YEAR CYCLES

* * * * * * * * * * * * * * * * *

NATURE IS GOVERNED by cycles; major cycles like birth and death, and smaller cycles like the phases of the moon, or the pattern of the day, which we measure by the 24-hour clock (which is made up of two 12-hour cycles). When you hear the saying that some people are in tune with life, this means that they are aware of the cycles around them and are therefore able to make the most of their potential. For example, a successful farmer who grows crops will know the best time to plant, and the best possible time to harvest each particular crop. The farmer may be only too aware of weather patterns and watch out for signs of weather that can have a positive or adverse affect over his produce. The farmer may also be totally in tune with the seasonal cycles and even the moon cycles too. However, some years the farmer may have a bumper crop and other years his yield may be smaller or even futile, because each year is influenced by a different vibration and pattern from the Universal or Collective Year Number.

RIGHT If you are in Personal Year Cycle 6, you may identify with facing deeper levels of commitment in your relationship.

UNIVERSAL YEAR CYCLES

You live in a world where you are ultimately aligned to the Universal or Collective Year Cycles, aptly named because these energies influence the collective, or whole of humanity. These numbers change every year according to the date. Although as an individual you are influenced by your own personal numbers in your chart, the larger cycle in life always has the greater say.

Universal Year Cycles remind you that you belong to a larger group or consciousness and encourage you to be flexible and make the most out of each day, even if it doesn't go the way you planned. They also remind you to step out of yourself sometimes and to see the bigger

ABOVE If your Personal Year Cycle 3 matches your Life Path Number 3 your natural talent for writing may intensify and may even prove lucrative.

picture in life. Indeed, people who are successful in their career, for example, are often aligned to these larger cycles and aware that taking an overall view of life can help them make the most out of their own potential.

To work out the current Universal Year Cycle you simply add up the current year you are in; 1999, for example, adds up to a 1 (you add $1 + 9 + 9 + 9 = 28$; $2 + 8 = 10$; $1 + 0 = 1$). So in the year 1999 everyone is influenced by the number 1 (and its sub-influences which are the 2 and the 8), with the qualities it brings. In the year 2000 you will be influenced by the number 2, and so on.

You are also influenced by the collective month cycles (1 – 12), week cycles (1 – 52), and daily cycles (1 – 7), although these have a less potent influence than the Universal Year Cycles. You may also like to work out a universal date, for example, July 18 1999, which adds up to $7 + 1 + 8 + 1 + 9 + 9 = 44$; $4 + 4 = 8$, to observe some of the qualities collectively influencing the world on that day. In the case of 8, one of its qualities is to highlight the need to balance the spiritual and the material elements within life, so issues surrounding this may arise that day.

PERSONAL YEAR CYCLES

When you are observing these Personal Year Cycles it is helpful to know the most important numbers in your numerology chart; when one of these numbers is highlighted within your Personal Year (or your Univeral Year) the qualities or issues associated with these numbers is intensified. For example, if your Life Path Number is a 3, and you enter a 3 Personal Year, then if one of your strengths is writing you may find that you write abundantly during that specific year. Or if one of your challenges is a lack of focus, then in a 3 year you may become even more unfocused, or the 3 energy may actually help you to refocus your energies.

Sometimes, during a specific Personal Year you may remember events, situations, or lessons you were learning the last time you were influenced by the same number. For example, if you were married in a 6 Personal Year and this was a happy event, then in your next 6 cycle you may feel like rekindling your energies or committing yourself even further to your relationship. Perhaps issues that challenge your commitment arise during the 6 cycle too.

To work out your Personal Year Cycle you simply add the day and the month of your birth to the year of your last birthday. So for example, if you were born on April 23 1983, your month of birth is 4 and your day of birth is 23, so 23 + 4 = 27. Then you add up the year of your last birthday. If today is February 14 2000, then your last birthday was in 1999 because you haven't had your birthday yet, so you add up 1 + 9 + 9 + 9 = 28. Then add them all together: 28 (the year) + 27 (the day and month) = 55, 5 + 5 = 1. Your current Personal Year Cycle is a 1.

Each of the cycles 1 to 9 highlight general meanings. For example, the years 1 to 6 focus on the physical experiences you are working through in life, while the 7th cycle highlights a synthesis of the previous 6 cycles. During the 8th and 9th cycles you are ending the 9-Year cycle; the 8th is associated with rebirth and the 9 highlights transformation as you complete one cycle and start another. All these cycles can help influence your health, career, relationships, and other experiences.

You may also like to work out your Personal Month or Week Cycles too, although (as with the Universal monthly and weekly cycles) they have less of an influence than the greater Personal Year Cycles. To work out your Personal Month Number, add the current month number (for example, November is the 11th month) to your current Personal Year Number. So if today's month is January (1) and your Personal Year Number is a 7, then 1 + 7 = 8, so your Personal Month Cycle for this January is an 8.

To work out your Personal Week Number, simply add the current week number to your current Personal Year Number. For example, in week 52 and a Personal Year Cycle 6, 5 + 2 + 6 = 13; 1 + 3 = 4, so your Personal Week Number works out to be a 4.

LEFT A Universal Number reveals qualities that collectively influence the world on that day, ranging from spiritual to material elements.

PERSONAL YEAR
AND UNIVERSAL YEAR NUMBERS

✦ ✦ ✦ ✦ ✦ ✦ ✦ ✦ ✦ ✦ ✦ ✦ ✦ ✦ ✦ ✦ ✦

THIS LIST HIGHLIGHTS some of the issues or situations that may be significant on a personal or collective level during each specific cycle.

Number 1

During a 1 Year you may find that life seems to take on a new direction in some way, or you may even feel stuck and feel unable to find your way ahead at times. Sometimes, before you can move forward, all the dead wood needs to be cleared always, so things may seem to break down or get worse for a while. For example, if you take up some form of new exercise during this 1 cycle, then you may feel aches and pains in your body, or even feel like giving up, because it seems too challenging. Indeed, it may collectively feel like a time of growing pains on either the physical, emotional, mental, or spiritual levels.

ABOVE People with a strong desire to move house may be reacting to a Personal Year 1 which highlights new beginnings.

Number 2

During a 2 Year you are working toward finding a balance in life. For example, this may be as a nation, balancing finances, or as an individual balancing the time you spend at work or with your family. Issues may arise this year to show you those areas that are out of balance. This 2 Year also highlights co-operation, though you may find that certain people, whether representatives of themselves or their country, may not want to compromise, and this may contribute toward creating imbalances in their own lives and within the world.

RIGHT During a Year 3 Cycle, your natural flair as an entertainer may blossom, as this cycle represents self-expression.

Number 3

Self-expression is highlighted during this 3 cycle; by being able to express your own inner self out to the world it can help your life to flow. Problems can be avoided by simple self-expression in business, politics, and within every area of daily life. When self-expression is held back, this causes energy to stagnate and prevents life from expanding and moving forward in its own natural way. This cycle is therefore asking you to be positive with your expression, as upbeat thoughts and actions contribute to a brighter future for everyone.

Number 4

During a 4 Year you are learning to take responsibility for yourself. You may find that you have a conflict of responsibilities in your life this year, or that you take on so many duties that you have insufficient energy to give them all your full attention. Life is still teaching you to take responsibility for having created these obligations in the first place. There may be a feeling of heaviness at times during this cycle, and you may realize the part you play in taking responsibility for the collective issues that arise in the world. For example, you may make changes to your lifestyle in order to take greater care of the environment.

Number 5

The 5 Year asks you to learn to communicate and to keep communicating so that the free flow of energy can continue upon this wonderful planet. During a 5 year you may find that you question your own life and lifestyle, or question issues arising in the world at large. As questions are asked, answers are supplied, and this can mean sudden changes as your overall viewpoint may change during this 5 cycle. Indeed, life may seem uncertain at times this year. Life is constantly changing, and this year may test your abilities to be adaptable to change.

Number 6

During a 6 Year issues surrounding the global community may be highlighted, such as social concerns that influence you personally and collectively. You may also find issues within your relationships become more intense this year as you either go deeply into exploring them, or you glamorize them or refuse to look at them. During this 6 Year you may find that you become more sensitive to those around you and to others' needs. Perhaps you feel neglected by those close to you, or by society; this may be very real, but it may also arise because your emotional sensitivity is heightened during this Number 6 Year.

Number 7

During a 7 Year you may find that you develop a more spiritual outlook on life or that you want to find out the meaning of life, and deeper issues in life may be highlighted collectively during this 7 cycle. You may find that you are introspective about the experiences that have occurred during the last 6 years. Individually and collectively the events of the last 6 years culminate at this stage in the cycle, and whether this time is more productive or less so, on one level or another, depends upon the lessons you have learned in previous cycles.

Number 8

During this year the whole world is strongly influenced by karma, and you may be aware of this in your own life. For example, situations from the past, which may have seemed resolved at the time, may arise. You may also feel an urge to become complete with the past. During a karmic period lessons to be learned usually feel very powerful indeed. Collectively or individually, these times allow for new growth, as you take the lessons you have learned from the past and move on.

Number 9

During this 9 Year life may seem to go through a transformation in preparation for the new 9-year cycle ahead. At times it may feel like you are in limbo, as you move from one complete 9-year cycle to the next. For example, legislation may have been agreed to improve the environment of the world in some way, but it has not yet been officially implemented. Issues that arise in this in-between stage may feel like they last forever, but learn to accept that each day is a part of the process of moving forward. Make the most of today!

ABOVE During a Personal Year 7 you may become more introspective about life.

NUMBER SEQUENCES

★ ★ ★ ★ ★ ★ ★ ★ ★ ★ ★ ★ ★ ★ ★ ★ ★

IN NUMEROLOGY YOUR Personality and Life Path Numbers are two of the most significant numbers in your chart because they combine to play a major role in the lessons you need to learn, and therefore the types of experiences you will have in your life. This is followed closely by your Soul Number, and your Karma or Wisdom Number. When you write down your own personal chart containing these numbers, translating your names into numbers derived from their position in the alphabet (A = 1, B = 2, C = 3 and so on), you will see that certain number sequences arise.

Perhaps one number is dominant in your full names on your birth certificate, for example the number 5, or you have lots of 1s in your date of birth. When one number reappears often, its qualities can be a positive attribute or are so intensified that they become a great challenge or teach you a great deal about your life. On the other hand, you may find that certain numbers are missing from your full names, and they may turn up in your Personality or Life Path Numbers or in your whole date of birth. Some may not feature in your chart at all (however, as you will see below, these omitted numbers can be just as important). Absent numbers can indicate that qualities need to be brought out and developed, and that you need to concentrate on them more strongly, but they can also mean that you have worked with them already and therefore you don't need to learn about these qualities. You can also see how many letters are in each of your names, and in all your names together, which will give you more information about numbers that are influencing your life.

It is very helpful to identify which number sequences are strong or omitted from your chart, because they give you a clue as to the lessons which need to be learned and potential issues which may arise, particularly when these numbers arise during a Personal Year Cycle.

BELOW Plotting your own chart is both exciting and revealing.

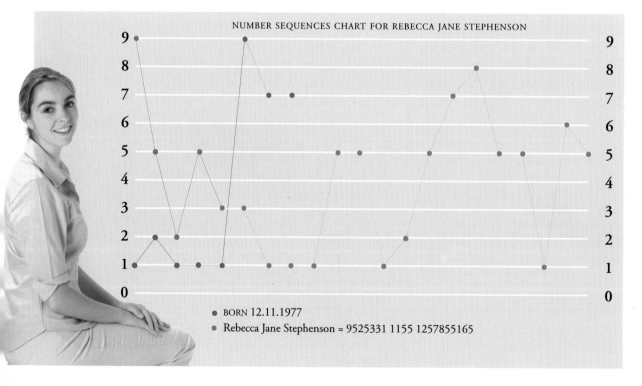

NUMBER SEQUENCES CHART FOR REBECCA JANE STEPHENSON

● BORN 12.11.1977
● Rebecca Jane Stephenson = 9525331 1155 1257855165

CASE STUDY

REBECCA JANE STEPHENSON BORN 12.11.1977

Personality Number 12/3
Life Path Number 11/2
Month of Birth 11/2

Rebecca Jane Stephenson = 21/3 letters
9525331 1155 1257855165

When you look at Rebecca's chart you will see
that her full names have 21 letters, which add
up to a 3, her Personality Number is a 3,
and that out of 21 letters in her name she
has another two 3s, and eight 5s. The
numbers 3 and 5 highlight self-expression and
communication so she may be brilliant with these
attributes or she may find it a challenge and a struggle
to express herself in the world at times. Perhaps she is
extrovert, bubbly, fun-loving, and vivacious too.

Her Life Path Number is an 11/2, and her month
number is an 11, and she has five 1s in her full names,
along with a 1 in her Personality Number. With all
these 1s Rebecca may be very ambitious, go-getting,
and highly energetic, but she may also resist being
direct with people in her life or aim for her own
personal goals at times.

The missing number from her names is a 4, which
fails to appear in her date of birth as well, so learning
about responsibility is one of her major lessons,
although if she has done this in the past, then this
transforms into a gift she can utilize.

CASE STUDY

CLARE MARIE JOHNSON BORN 17.6.1963
33195 41995 16851665

In Clare's chart, based upon the full names on her birth certificate, the first letter of her first name starts with a 3 and the last letter of her last name ends with a 5, highlighting communication and self-expression as some of her potential gifts and her lessons in life. Half of the numbers in her names lie between the numbers 4 and 6, which may mean that she is quite a responsible person who enjoys living in the physical world, and enjoys having fun and also the good things in life.

There are, however, quite a few highs and lows, but their paths are broken by the numbers between 4 and 6, which may add a cushioning influence. On the other hand, this may signify an inner fear of reaching the highest of highs and the lowest of lows and at times she may fear experiencing life to the full.

Clare's date of birth begins on a 1 and ends on a 3. Perhaps she is a keen individual and quite bright and intellectual too, as both these numbers have aspects pertaining to the mind. Her upper and lower lines are cushioned by the number 6, so it may signify her ability to rely on her instincts to get her through life to some degree.

When you look at your own chart you may not recognize patterns at first, but after a while something may jump out to teach you a little more about your life. You can also ask someone close to you to look at your graph to mirror back how they interpret the energy or qualities of the numbers. You can also add other details into your graph, such as each of your individual names, your time of birth, or the name of the place or country in which you were born. You can also find out numerological information about the numbers in your chart from other chapters in this book, particularly the chapter on the Personality and Life Path Numbers. Numbers are fascinating and fun, and by drawing these numerological graphs you can learn to play with numbers in a very powerful way.

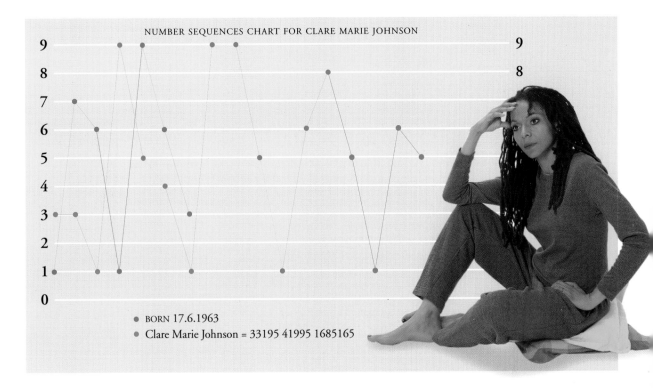

NUMBER SEQUENCES CHART FOR CLARE MARIE JOHNSON

● BORN 17.6.1963
● Clare Marie Johnson = 33195 41995 1685165

OBSERVING NUMBER SEQUENCES IN YOUR CHART

Look at your own chart and make a note of which numbers are in abundance and which are missing, and then look up those numbers in the chart below. Remember that these numbers appear to indicate your personal strengths, but that they also contain challenges and should be read as a way of helping you to learn important lessons in life.

NUMBER QUALITIES

1 independence, direction, ambition

2 wisdom, compassion, co-operation

3 self-expression, mental activity, focus

4 responsibility, loyalty, determination

5 communication, adventure, perception

6 wholeness, commitment, sensitivity

7 intuition, imagination, productivity

8 spiritual and material balance, power, authority

9 inner knowledge, inspiration, freedom

YOUR PERSONAL GRAPH

When you draw out your personal date of birth and names you can see the sequence the numbers follow and how the flow of the numbers influences you in your life. For example, you can see if your first name begins with a low number and ends with a high number, or if it begins with a high number and ends with a low number or somewhere in between. Perhaps your chart shows that you are quite placid, with many of the numbers around the same height in your chart, or you might have a dramatic chart, indicating great highs and extreme lows.

When you interpret your Personal Graph by applying your own inner wisdom, information about how to use or apply your energy in your daily life is revealed. Can you see where your life flows, the blockages, the overall gifts? You can compare your graph with those of loved ones, or important people, so that you can observe how your energies correspond together. Remember, this is not a logical process for you to analyse every number to perfection; rather, this should help you to get a feel for the flow of your overall chart.

ABOVE Clare's chart exposes her natural gift for acting, communication, self-expression, and need for personal challenges.

53

YOUR NUMEROLOGY FAMILY TREE

* * * * * * * * * * * * * * * *

NUMEROLOGY IS PARTICULARLY useful when you want to find out more about who you are from your family tree. A numerology tree can also help to give you a bigger picture of issues that have influenced your family, perhaps throughout generations. Karmic issues also show up in your physiological DNA, and these can be traced back biologically through this numerology tree.

Sometimes by studying your numerology tree you may also be encouraged to resolve old patterns of behavior or to let go of past family feuds. For example, if your great-grandparents were feuding with your grandparents, you are able to highlight the issue numerologically. If you have the same number in your chart, you may recognize that issue yourself and may even come to resolve it. Perhaps you can see what your relatives were needing to learn and can release the need to experience that specific situation or behavior again.

A numerology tree is also helpful when you rub up against a (perhaps distant) member of your family and you wish to find out why. Perhaps you again have the same numbers in your date of birth, or you even share the same name, or the same numbers in your names. It may be that their soul, for example, is teaching your Personality something important, and through numbers in the tree you may find out what it is and why.

Working through your numerology tree with another member of your family can also be a wonderful healing process, because you can learn together and share your views and feelings about what is revealed. You may discover talents that have long since lapsed within your family, and if you have those same numbers in your chart you may choose to rekindle these family skills if you can. Perhaps you are brilliant at playing the harp, and by looking back you may see where this musical gift comes from. If you were adopted as a child, then working out your adopted family's tree can provide information about the role you play within their family, and possibly why they chose you to be a part of their group family.

At certain critical times in your life, particularly when you are going through transformation and change, you may wish to consider your family roots in your numerology tree. It may give you strength, particularly if you are able to feel the spiritual connection in the continuation of life through past generations, and it may help to put your own life into greater perspective.

You can work on a numerology tree with the family you were born into, and also for your own children and extended family. It is fascinating to see the influence a marriage partner can bring into the family. If you have children but are not married, you can still draw up a tree, though the family name or surname may be different for the mother, the father, or the child if different partners are involved. It may be a revealing, if complex, process to observe the energies and qualities being brought into the family collective by all the different people of your group.

RIGHT By studying your numerology family tree, you may discover a unique inherited gift, such as a good musical ear.

ABOVE Relatives face tensions but, in time, former family discords may be resolved by new generations tracing their numerological family tree.

CAITKIN SAMANTHA BROWN,
BORN 14.4.1984.

Personality Number	14/5
Life Path Number	45/9
Soul Number	28/10/1
Childhood Number	53/8
Karma Number	81/9
First Name	31/4
Middle Name	23/5
Family Name	27/9
Age	15/6
Personal Year	25/7

CAITKIN'S MOTHER,
SAMANTHA MARY SMITH,
BORN 8.9.1960. HER MARRIED NAME IS BROWN.

Personality Number	8
Life Path Number	33/6
Soul Number	20/2
Childhood Number	48/12/3
Karma Number	68/14/5
First Name	23/5
Middle Name	21/3
Family Name	24/6
Married Name	27/9
Age	40/4
Personal Year	19/10/1

CAITKIN'S FATHER, DAVID BROWN
(NO MIDDLE NAME),
BORN 7.7.1957.

Personality Number	7
Life Path Number	36/9
Soul Number	16/7
Childhood Number	33/6
Karma Number	49/13/4
First Name	22/4
Family Name	27/9
Age	43/7
Personal Year	16/7

LEFT Tracing your numerological family can be exciting.

RIGHT Caitkin's Childhood Number and her mother Samantha's Personality Number are the same, Number 8. This highlights potential compatabilities, but there could also be power struggles.

CHARTING OUT YOUR NUMEROLOGY FAMILY TREE

In order to map out your numerology tree you first need to chart out your date of birth and full names on your birth certificate, writing down all the major numbers which are in your numerology chart: these are the Personality, Life Path, Soul, Childhood, and Karma Numbers. Then write down your age and your Personal Year Numbers, to highlight influences over your current year. You may also like to add up each of your individual First, Middle, and Family Name Numbers, as well as your Marriage Name, to highlight other important aspects of your chart.

Next, as you would chart out a regular family tree, map out your relatives' details onto the page, particularly those who are immediate family or close to you. If you were raised by grandparents instead of your parents, you may see a strong connection between you because you have the same numbers, or see why this was so. You may not have all of your family's dates of birth, or even their full names, but everything in their chart is relevant.

IMPORTANT DATES

When you are looking at the overall Tree, you may be able to work out important family dates from the past, such as birth dates, marriage dates, or death dates. If you know their dates of birth, then you can work out their Personal and Universal Year Numbers to understand more about the timing of these events and perhaps the lessons involved.

You continue working out as much information as you can about the numbers in your relatives' charts, then apply it to a map on a separate page with all your major numbers written down.

You can see from Caitkin's chart that her

Personality Number 5 is the same as her mother's First Name and Karma Number; these highlight possible areas of compatibility and also challenges if they rub up against each other. Number 5 highlights communication which may flow between them, or it may be an issue. Perhaps Samantha works as a journalist or writer and Caitkin wants to follow in her footsteps. Caitkin's Childhood Number is also the same as her mother's Personality Number 8, so there may be power struggles between them.

Caitkin and her father have the same Life Path Number 9, although the sub-influences are different, which means that they may share their bigger vision of the world at large. They may both be interested in cultural events and

LEFT By mapping every aspect of their respective numerological charts, Caitkin and her mother may learn to reconcile their differences.

also be musical or artistic. Caitkin and her father in addition have the same number 4 for their First Names, but once again with different sub-influences. Caitkin may therefore have a similar outlook on life for material concerns, or they may both have issues to confront about responsibility.

Drawing Conclusions

This case history simply highlights a few simple numbers and qualities for you to understand how to work out your own Tree. You can carry on making connections with all the members of your family, going back for generations.

It is always helpful to work with facts, so finding out about your relatives by talking to them can be very helpful. You can use your intuition to guide you, too. Indeed, nobody sees the same person in quite the same way, therefore all life is subjective and open to interpretation, and therefore makes all the experiences unique. Open up your mind and allow the numbers to sink deep into your subconscious so that they can reveal what they need to.

LEFT The more dates of birth and names you have, the more extensive your numerology family tree becomes!

YOUR CHART AS A WHOLE

* * * * * * * * * * * * * * * *

IT IS HUMAN nature to want to find out more about yourself and what makes you tick. In numerology you can find out a great deal about your life from your chart.

RIGHT There are many aspects to numbers, but they are all intrinsically connected because they represent life.

In numerology, particularly when you are becoming aware of numbers for the first time, you may find that you see all the different aspects of your chart as separate energies influencing your life. But you are unique, and the way all your numbers interact together and influence you collectively is what is really important. You can still be influenced more by one number at any time. For example, your Personality Number may play a more significant role in your life in your 20s than your Life Path Number.

Therefore it is essential to be able to stand back from your Numerology chart and to let it form a pattern in your mind so that the overall chart speaks to you. You will generally need to know some of the basic qualities contained within each number and to find out the roles the numbers play in your life, particularly the major numbers like your Personality, Life Path, Soul, Childhood, and Karma Numbers. Sometimes you may find that if you open your mind to numbers they reveal information, even when you have not learned about the qualities or attributes they contain.

It can be very helpful to get feedback about your chart from loved ones so that they can channel information back to you, but it is possible to take an overall view of your chart even if it comes in a less objective way than comments from others. Every time you look at your chart you bring a fresh eye, because you are changing each day and therefore bring to it a new perspective. You can go through your whole lifetime reading your numerology chart, and the numbers will continue to reveal more jewels of information.

When you observe one of the areas of your chart, such as your Life Path Number, you may find that you do not identify with some of the attributes it contains. This can arise for many reasons. Firstly, you may be more influenced by your Personality Number or some other number in your chart at that specific time. Secondly, you may be too close to yourself to recognize the qualities within yourself, or may not want to see some of them. Thirdly, each number flows into the next; therefore every number in your chart contains elements of the number preceding and following it. For example, if you have a 23/5 Personality Number influencing you, then the qualities and potential of the numbers 22/4 and 24/6 will also influence you to a lesser degree, though the number 23/5 will have the most significance in your life. These flowing energies from other numbers can also be stronger at specific times in your life. Finally these qualities may be "hidden" or unrecognized by you to date.

Each number contains within its potential elements of all the other numbers that have gone before it. For example, the number 23/5 as a Personality Number means that to some degree the numbers 1 to 22 have been encountered or learned about before. You may also go back to another number to relearn more about it, and you may also attract people who have that number strongly present in their chart too. So with a 23/5 Personality Number you may attract a person to you with the number 9, for example, if this is something which needs to be relearned, or you may in your next lifetime be born with a number 9 Personality Number.

Looking at the overall picture can mean that you get a clearer picture of yourself and the different possibilities that are open to you in your life, particularly when you take the larger picture, the collective, into consideration too. For example, you may observe that many people in life are currently becoming computer literate. So, if you find a 5 in your chart, which is associated with communication and computers, you may think it's potentially a good time to train to become a computer programmer, because you are observant of the bigger cycles in life, and how they can influence your own personal numerology chart. Of course, numerology helps you to develop and become more attuned to your intuition, as it opens you up to deeper aspects within yourself. Looking at your potential in life is easier when you can see the whole picture.

CASE STUDY

JEAN PAUL BROWN BORN 19.4.1971

Personality Number 19/10 = 1
Life Path Number   41 = 5
Soul Number   16 = 7
Childhood Number 37/10 = 1
Karma   53 = 8

PERSONALITY NUMBER 19/10/1

Jean may be direct, ambitious, lively, creative, and really enjoy pursuing his goals. He may love to lead, but be very independent and in fear of getting too close to people at times.

LIFE PATH NUMBER 41/5

Jean may be very grounded, practical, and ambitious, but his restlessness may mean that he does not always finish what he starts. He may be a good communicator.

SOUL NUMBER 16/7

His soul is asking him to go inside and refine his intuition, which is probably already polished to some degree.

CHILDHOOD NUMBER 37/10/1

Jean may have been very focused as a child and very creative; perhaps he was always making things with his hands.

KARMA NUMBER 53/8

In the past Jean may have been a real instigator who led others through the battlefield and fought for victory and success.

OVERALL CHART

You can see that the number 1 seems to play a strong role in influencing his life right now, with ambition, drive, and focus. You can see that he may also have strong leadership skills from this number and also from the numbers 8 and 9. However, he may be a little bossy (8s) at times because he is willful (1) and stubborn, so he may not like his path to be crossed. Indeed, he may know what he wants in life, and he communicates this (from the 5s in his Soul and Karma Numbers) and, with the 4s in his Life Path, ensures he achieves his goals (1s).

Overall, in this chart lots of the digits contain mental energy, so he may be very intellectual and need to open up to his emotions sometimes. He may also be a bit of a charmer (8) with a good sense of humor (3s and 9s), and be a sweet-talker, too (5s).

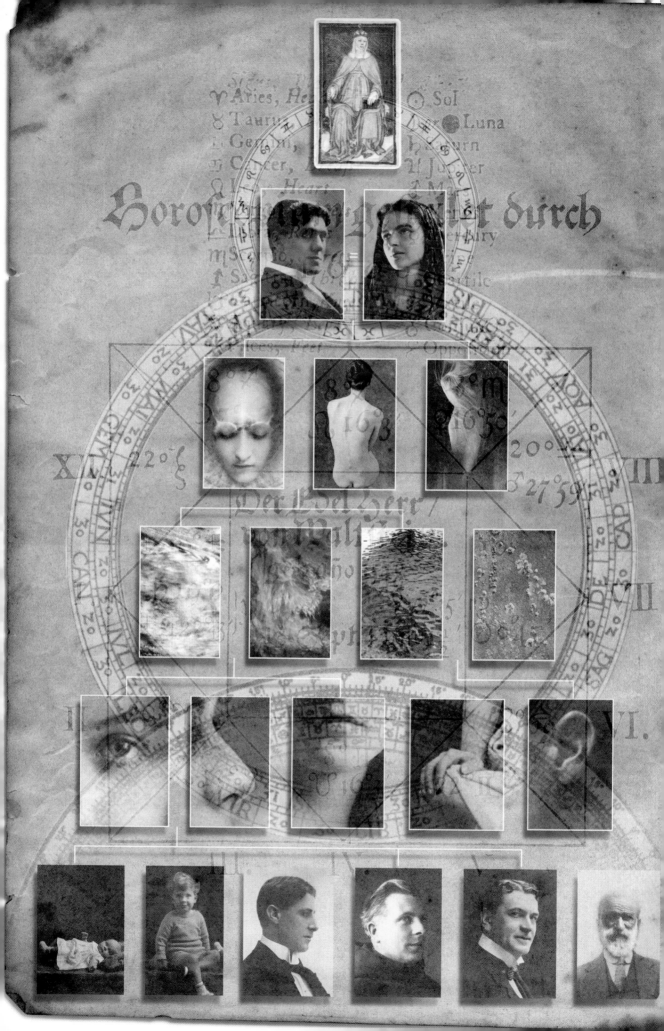

PART TWO

YOU AND YOUR RELATIONSHIPS

★ ★ ★ ★ ★

Your relationship with yourself is the most significant relationship of all, and this determines what sort of people and situations you attract. Ultimately, relating to your inner self influences the kind of relationships you make and create with others in your life.

Everyone has elements within themselves which they are particularly working with during each lifetime – physical, emotional, mental, and spiritual elements. At times you work on some levels more than on others, and this can influence how you relate to the people around you. Sometimes you may feel connected to a person mentally, and at others you may connect emotionally.

ABOVE Attraction between two people stems from each person striving to learn about the physical, emotional, mental, or spiritual elements of life.

Numerology helps you to make the most of all your relationships by bringing awareness of your potential, your strengths, and the challenges you face. You can also grow wise from the knowledge that everything in life is intrinsically connected.

THE BIGGER NUMBERS: 1–81

* * * * * * * * * * * * * * * * * *

WHEN YOU ARE looking through this book you may want more information about the larger numbers. Part One covers this in brief, discussing Personality Numbers 1 to 31. However, when you are working out other numbers, for example your Life Path Number or your Karma Number (or other numbers which crop up in life in general), this can help you to understand a little about how these numbers may influence you. Each number has an infinite amount of associated qualities and listed below are but a few to spark off your own inner wisdom about the nature of each number.

Every number in your chart, and in life, eventually adds up to a digit between 1 to 9, and these energies are the strongest because they are condensed. But the other digits contained within the larger numbers are also important sub-influences too, bringing additional strengths, challenges, and lessons. For example, a 27/9 has a strong influence from the qualities of the 9, but the 7 and the 2 also influence this number and influence your life.

The 7 and 2 are sub-influences of the number 9, which help to finely tune the potential contained within the final digit. 2 and 7 are watery numbers and the 9 has strong spiritual energy, so you would expect sensitivity when this 27/9 number is influencing life.

Here are some general trends contained within all the numbers 1 to 81, which has been chosen as the final digit, because when 9 (the last

number in the 1 to 9 cycle) is multiplied by 9 it adds up to 81, but you can continue counting infinitely. Also included are the numbers 1 to 9, so that you have the full 81 cycle of numbers for reference.

1 Number 1 highlights: new beginnings, finding your own path direction, going for goals, and focusing on life. You may be angry and destructive at times.

2 Number 2 highlights: the need to find love, to learn to share, to have compassion, and to find harmony in life. You can also be overemotional and cold.

3 This 3 energy highlights: fun, joy, activity, response, laughter, and the need to learn to express yourself. You can also be scattered and unfocused.

4 Number 4 highlights: passion, creativity, determination, and the need to keep your feet on the ground. You may also feel insecure on occasions.

5 The 5 energy highlights: a bright, quick, and perceptive mind, common sense, sensuality, fun, and the need to communicate. You may also be unpredictable.

6 Number 6 highlights: the need to serve or to help others, to nurture yourself, generosity, warmth, love, and affection. You may also get carried away and be self-indulgent sometimes.

RIGHT Number 4; you may be down-to-earth, resilient, and passionate.

BELOW Physical strength and focusing the mind are qualities contained within the Number 2.

7 Number 7 highlights: spirituality, sensitivity, intuition, vision, and the need to be productive and to instigate change. However, you may sometimes be gullible or get lost in your emotions.

8 Number 8 highlights: power, materialism, and a strong need to re-evaluate life, even on a daily basis. You could at times be taken in by your own power, or like to control others.

9 Number 9 highlights: humor, creativity, education, a need for an open mind, and the ability to be adaptable to life. Be aware that you may be also selfish and prudish at times.

10/1 The 10/1 energy highlights: wisdom, knowledge, vitality, and the need to get ahead with your creative gifts and ambition. Sometimes you may be self-centered and stubborn.

11/2 Number 11/2 highlights: passion, highly creative nervous energy, intense feelings, and a need to bring harmony and balance into your life. Unrealistic expectations may mean disappointments too.

12/3 This 12/3 energy highlights: ambition, drive, productivity, warmth, and caring, with a need for self-expression. However, you can also be over-fussy and exacting.

13/4 Number 4 highlights: drama, risk-

taking, insecurity, spiritual growth, new opportunities, and a need to take on responsibility. You may sometimes be overemotional and impractical.

14/5 Number 14/5 highlights: wisdom, inner knowledge, magnetism, vitality, and a need to communicate and to connect with life. You may be dreamy and think too much.

15/6 Number 15/6 highlights: sensitivity, sensuality, motivation, love, compassion, and a need to learn to listen to what people say. You may be driven to satisfy only your own desires at times.

16/7 The 16/7 energy highlights: an intellectual mind, introspection, love, affection, and a need to learn to relax and to trust the process of life. You may sometimes be overanalytical.

17/8 Number 17/8 highlights: karma, a strong will, mental stimulation, spirituality, and a desire to seek out a deeper meaning to life. You may also be stubborn.

18/9 Number 18/9 highlights: leadership, direct communication, selflessness, humor, and a need to discriminate. You may also be judgmental and indulge in power struggles.

ABOVE Number 10/1 highlights the need to check your stubborn streak.

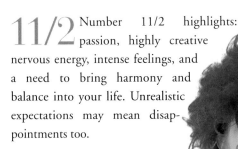

LEFT Number 3; clowning around comes naturally, and is a positive means of self-expression.

19/10/1 The 19/10/1 energy highlights: inspiration, strong and powerful leadership, humanitarian interests, ambition, and individuality. You may sometimes be forceful and self-righteous.

20/2 Number 20/2 highlights: a need to weigh things up, to feel through the instincts, to relate to people and to life, and to be able to share with others. You may also be very moody sometimes.

21/3 Number 21/3 highlights: joy, abundance, optimism, creativity, inspiration, light-heartedness, and the social aspects of life. You may sometimes be scattered and lack direction or purpose.

22/4 Number 22/4 highlights: balance, harmony, emotional connection, diplomacy, consideration, and responsibility. You may also feel great inner conflicts or be confrontational at times.

23/5 This 23/5 energy highlights: sensuality, joy, adventure, an uplifting nature, expression, and a highly developed mind. You may also get lost in your imagination sometimes.

24/6 Number 24/6 highlights: a need to provide for others, time management, devotion, commitment, and a need for security. You may also romanticize life at times.

25/7 Number 25/7 highlights: adventure, movement, communication, observation, intuition, and common sense. You may also be ruled by your head, or cut off from your emotions at times.

26/8 The 26/8 energy highlights: sensitivity to others' needs, a need to be needed, support, care, glamor, and comfort. You may also become too emotionally attached to people at times.

27/9 Number 27/9 highlights: simplicity, honesty, openness, vulnerability, commitment, and a need to be right or wrong about life. You may sometimes feel emotionally fragile.

28/10/1 Number 28/10/1 highlights: ambition, business flair, creative ideas, vitality, and a need to be assertive. You may sometimes impose your will upon others.

29/11/2 This 29/11/2 energy highlights: magnetism charm, inspiration, intuition, knowledge, and a need to set fair standards. You may also be intense and emotionally demanding.

BELOW Glamor and living in a social whirl may suit those who have a 30/3 in their chart.

35/8 Number 35/8 highlights: re-evaluation, strength, courage, power, communication, perception, activity, magnetism, and charm. You may also feel that your freedom is restricted at times (or you may impose this on yourself).

36/9 Number 36/9 highlights: human-itarian interests, selflessness, social awareness, sensitivity, and sentimentality. You may also have the tendency to be over-giving and perhaps emotionally smothering at times.

37/10/1 The 37/10/1 energy highlights: vision, focus, the will to follow through on ideas, exhibition-ism, spirituality, and hypersensitivity. You may sometimes feel isolated or cut yourself off from others.

38/11/2 Number 38/11/2 highlights: dynamic will, ambition, determination, charm, humor, receptivity, and gentleness. You can also be pushy, stubborn, and aggressive at times.

39/12/3 This 39/12/3 highlights: a laid-back, happy-go-lucky atti-tude to life and a need for self-acceptance. You may want to sometimes be "carried" instead of taking responsibility for yourself.

40/4 Number 40/4 high-lights: earthiness, solidity, structure, responsibility, passion, and loyalty. Sometimes you may be indecisive about your goals in life.

30/3 Number 30/3 highlights: flexibil-ity, abundant self-expression, the need to talk, fun and entertainment, activity, and generosity. You may feel resentment toward life at times.

31/4 Number 31/4 highlights: will power, endurance, commitment, efficiency, focused attention, and communica-tion. You may also be attention-seeking or feel insecure at times.

32/5 Number 32/5 highlights: a sunny nature, freedom, self-expression, variety, fascination, and an enquiring mind. You may at times run around so much your feet don't touch the ground.

33/6 Number 33/6 highlights: a need to support, to help, and to serve others, self-sacrifice, wisdom, team spirit, appre-ciation, and joy. You may also feel the conflict of responsibilities at times.

34/7 Number 34/7 highlights: joy, happiness, expansion, freedom, responsibility, and a happy-go-lucky attitude. You could sometimes be irresponsible.

LEFT With a 23/5 you may be romantic and sensual.

BELOW The Greek myth "Atlas" is a poignant symbol of the 35/8: courage, strength, and submission.

ABOVE With a 42/6, you may enjoy organization, routine, and systems.

41/5 The 41/5 energy highlights: abundant communication, change, commitment, freedom, movement, and a need for stability. You may also be restless at times.

42/6 This 42/6 energy highlights: discipline, structure, love, sensitivity, wholeness, a passion for systems, and comfort. You may also be rigid in your need for routine sometimes.

43/7 The 43/7 energy highlights: organization, stability, faddishness, practicality, an analytical mind, attention to detail, introspection, and productiveness. You may sometimes be prone to having irrational outbursts.

44/8 Number 44/8 highlights: charm, power, strength, boundaries, and the ability to get on with life step by step. You may at times feel bogged down by your responsibilities in life.

45/9 This 45/9 energy highlights: education, knowledge, learning, teaching, discrimination, security, and a need for intellectual conversation. You may sometimes preach to others and are capable of being highly opinionated.

46/10/1 Number 46/10/1 highlights: a need for emotional and physical security, focus, direction, determination, warmth, generosity, service, and help to others. You may be too self-absorbed sometimes.

RIGHT With a Number 51/6, you may love trinkets and treasures.

47/11/2 Number 47/11/2 highlights: clarity, inspiration, vision, emotional sensitivity, materialism, and a need for co-operation. You may be too dreamy and get caught up in illusions at times.

48/12/3 Number 48/12/3 highlights: assertiveness, communication, expansion, organization, and a need to let life flow. You may also at times get easily frustrated with life.

49/13/4 This number 49/13/4 highlights: spontaneity, opportunities, boundaries, structure, will power, organization, education, and the need to achieve goals. You may find it difficult to communicate sometimes.

50/5 Number 50/5 highlights: spontaneity, fun, movement, magnetism, charm, commitment, and a need to communicate. You may also be addicted to life sometimes.

51/6 Number 51/6 highlights: justice, fairness, truth, glamor, courage, dynamic enthusiasm, will power, and a need to appreciate beauty. Your behaviour may be very changeable at times.

52/7 Number 52/7 highlights: introspection, communication, perception, intuition, clarity, warmth, common sense, and productivity. You may also feel too vulnerable sometimes.

53/8 Number 53/8 highlights: competence, flattery, powerful self-expression and leadership, inspiration, energy, levity, fun, entertainment, and also intellectual matters. You may sometimes deal with things by being verbally abusive.

54/9 Number 54/9 highlights: inner knowledge, wisdom, creativity, discussion, selflessness, power, confidence and liberality. You may also be resigned to helping others, but at other times be very selfish.

55/10/1 The 55/10/1 energy highlights: direction, opportunities, change, fresh ideas, new ways of thinking, with a need to express yourself to the world. You can sometimes be highly unpredictable and react in an explosive way toward others.

56/11/2 Number 56/11/2 highlights: passion, drive, gentleness, emotional stability, generosity, an urge toward perfectionism, together with a need for mental stimulation and conversation. You may also be temperamental or have the sulks periodically.

57/12/3 Number 57/12/3 highlights: expansion, joy, creative expression, business flair, productivity, humor, inspiration, and a need for introspection. You may sometimes be careless with your communication.

ABOVE The businesslike approach of Number 53/8 may be detected in a person's confident gesture.

58/13/4 Number 58/13/4 highlights: transformation, change, new opportunities, grounding, flexibility, spontaneity, and inner strength. You may find that dramas rule your life.

59/14/5 Number 59/14/5 highlights: communication, introspection, research, knowledge, adventure, perception, and magnetism. You may find that commitment in a particular relationship is sometimes a major challenge.

60/6 Number 60/6 highlights: protection, sensitivity, wholeness, generosity, and creativity, with a love for beauty and esthetics. You may be emotionally dependent upon others at times.

61/7 This 61/7 energy highlights: vision, intuition, focus, productivity, and wisdom, and you enjoy bringing people together and instigating things. You may at times be too withdrawn and introspective.

62/8 Number 62/8 highlights: business flair, competition, ambition, dedication, emotional support, and healing. You may sometimes be taken in by the glamor of success.

63/9 Number 63/9 highlights: love, affection, expression, sensuality, generosity, fun, joy, creativity, freedom, and commitment. You may also be scattered and confused at times.

64/10/1 Number 64/10/1 highlights: new opportunities, wisdom, leadership, wholeness, discipline, beauty, passion, and a need to serve and help others. You may at times also be naive.

65/11/2 This 65/11/2 energy highlights: inspiration, charm, magnetism, devotion, direction, care, diplomacy, and a need for harmony. Sometimes your occasional emotional outbursts might be rather destructive.

66/12/3 Number 66/12/3 highlights: expansion, communication, the need to serve others, idealism, sensuality, and a love of beauty. You may sometimes be jealous of others' looks or success.

67/13/4 Number 67/13/4 highlights: healing, wisdom, productivity, new opportunities, transformation, change, and the need to keep your feet on the ground. You may prefer to live in a dream world at times.

68/14/5 This 68/14/5 energy highlights: introspection, beauty, devotion, perfection, clarity, intellectual conversation, and authority. You may be unable to appreciate others points of view sometimes.

69/15/6 Number 69/15/6 highlights: instincts, emotional sensitivity, sensuality, spontaneity, persuasion, will power, focus, ambition, and a need to help others. You may sometimes be devious.

70/7 Number 70/7 highlights: fruition, completion, spirituality, intuition, protection, with a need for space to think and for introspection. You may be overprotective sometimes.

71/8 Number 71/8 highlights: success, strength, will power, relentless determination, enthusiasm, dynamic focus, and you enjoy bringing ideas into fruition. You may also be too materialistic at times and overly concerned with success.

72/9 Number 72/9 highlights: sensitivity, intuition, simplicity, honesty, openness, humor, and a need to please others and be accepted. You may also refuse to listen to others' wisdom at times.

73/10/1 Number 73/10/1 highlights: new opportunities, new vision, freedom, vitality, productivity, intuition, mysticism, with a need to trust your

BELOW Setting physically challenging feats goes hand in hand with the dynamic energies highlighted in the number 71/8.

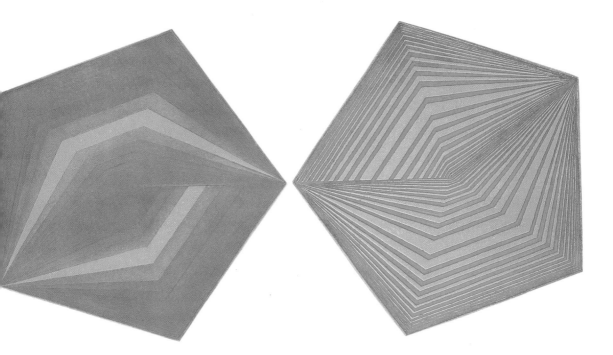

inner wisdom. At times you may feel full of your own self-importance.

74/11/2 The 74/11/2 energy highlights: appreciation, music, color, beauty, vision, intuition, naivety, and a need to feel secure. You may sometimes find yourself lacking motivation and develop a state of inertia.

75/12/3 Number 75/12/3 highlights: fluency in communication, physical expression, emotional sensitivity, magnetism, charm, spontaneity, and ambition. You may feel like running away from the chaos and confusion in your life sometimes.

76/13/4 Number 76/13/4 highlights: determination, harmony, comfort, wholeness, communication, and structure, You may really resist and struggle with life sometimes.

77/14/5 This 77/14/5 energy highlights: introspection, research, intuition, knowledge, self-expression, earthiness, demonstrativeness, and politeness. You may at times be very provocative in your speech.

78/15/6 Number 78/15/6 highlights: strength, ambition, comfort, emotional warmth, compassion, organization, and a need to love and feel good about yourself and others. You may, however, be insensitive to the needs of other people at times and only think of yourself.

79/16/7 This 79/16/7 energy highlights: imagination, spirituality, cultural interests, wholeness, productivity, and a need to search for the truth. You may at times dislike criticism and others judging you.

80/8 Number 80/8 highlights: leadership, empowerment, strength, spiritual will, charm, inspiration, organisation, and a need to balance the inner spiritual side and outer material aspects of life. You may be possessive both of your material goods and to those you are in relationship with sometimes.

81/9 Number 81/9 highlights: leadership, discrimination, transformation, new direction, humor, creativity, and a need to develop your mind. You might be really bossy at times and have a tendency to expect people to do what you want.

MASTER NUMBERS

★ ★ ★ ★ ★ ★ ★ ★ ★ ★ ★ ★ ★ ★ ★ ★ ★ ★

MASTER NUMBERS ARE found when digits are doubled; for example, 11, 22, 33, and so on. They can be found in any area of your chart. Perhaps you were born in the 11th month of November, or on the 22nd of the month, or perhaps your Life Path, Soul, Childhood, or Karma Numbers are made up of numbers that add up to a Master Number. Perhaps your Soul Number is a 29/11/2, or your Karma Number is a 65/11/2.

Each Master Number adds up to a digit, which always has the strongest influence over your life. For example, 22 adds up to a 4. Some people are significantly influenced by these Master Numbers and make the most of their potential. If you have a Master Number (or more than one) in your chart you are being made aware of gifts that can help others in the bigger world. They are not gifts to be used simply for yourself. Each digit is doubled and therefore amplifies the digit it mirrors, amplifying its strengths and its challenges. If you make the most of your gifts it can help you to be more successful with your life and incorporate this success to help others. (Of course, you can also be successful without Master Numbers in your chart.)

Having a Master Number can give you a clue to the direction you would like to head toward in life. For example, you may have a 33/6 as a Soul Number, which highlights service, looking after others, healing, and wisdom. You may then decide to take up a profession as a nurse, doctor, or, complimentary therapist or work within the caring professions. You may also have a gift for entertaining, and you may help others to feel good by brightening up their day with a dance, a song, or a joke, which is healing too.

A Master Number in your chart may be giving you a wake-up call to see if you can step outside of yourself and think of others in a big way. Some people with Master Numbers are aware of the value of goodwill, for example, and they practice this in their lives by giving to others. Indeed, you do not need to change your job in order to serve your community or the wider world. For example, you may choose to be more positive about life, which can influence everyone in your environment and contributes toward a more positive world.

Many people today are generally more open to the inner spiritual values of life. If you have Master Numbers in your chart, you may particularly find yourself looking for ways to take an active role in meeting the needs of the world in this new millennium.

ABOVE Master Numbers can offer clues as to your vocation in life.

RIGHT Master Numbers influence your potential gifts.

70

MASTER NUMBERS 11 TO 99

Consult your own numerology chart. If you have discovered your Master Numbers, then look them up below.

11/2 With a Master Number 11, you may possess a finely tuned intuition and an heightened sensitivity to life. You may therefore be driven to use these gifts through art, music, the theater or in the healing arts. Pioneering is also one of your gifts, and you may pave a new direction ahead for others. You may also appear intense and nervous, and feel superior at times.

22/4 With a Master Number 22, you may possess the gift of compassion, and you may also be a visionary who can easily see the bigger picture when others are bogged down with minor details. With clarity of vision, you may then take one step at a time in order to materialize your vision into reality. You may also be oversensitive and emotional, losing your footing for a while when laying foundations for others.

33/6 With a Master Number 33/6, you may easily be able to see the overall picture in any situation, and to instinctually feel others' needs. You radiate joy and compassion, and give freely to others. You may sometimes give too much and then feel guilty. Sometimes even when you have given generously to others, you may blame yourself for not giving enough.

44/8 With a Master Number 44/8, you may have a strong instinct for survival, with a get-up-and-go attitude that ensures you approach each day in a practical way. You may handle responsibility well, and be able to encourage others to do the same. You enjoy laying foundations that others can build upon. Sometimes you might be unreliable, or resist taking on responsibilities.

LEFT Whether you enjoy sculpting or painting, your ability to visualize the esthetic elements in life may be reinforced with Master Number 22/4.

BELOW Learn from your Master Number 33/6; balance your compassion and selflessness with an appreciation of your own needs.

ABOVE Master Number 55/10/1; talking and reading are ways of communicating with the world.

down by all the little details of everday life so that you lose your sense of the bigger picture. You may panic at times, and can lose your sense of reality.

88/16/7
With a Master Number 88/16/7, you may have a gift for handling power and authority in a positive way so others look to you to lead them. You may be an ideas person who can conjure up solutions to others' problems, and produce successful resolutions in no time at all. However, you may also find that at times you are dominating, controlling, and rigid in your approach to life.

55/10/1
With a Master Number 55/10/1, you may use your bright mind and your clear perception to lead others, particularly through situations of transformation and change. Your gift for communication may mean that you can easily represent others in many different ways, or even translate what people say for others to hear. Sometimes you may be inconsistent with your communication, and are apt to being very changeable at times.

99/18/9
With a Master Number 99/18/9, you may have a gift for inspiring others with your creativity, particularly with art and music. You may also be knowledgeable in current affairs and outspoken in your opinions. You may also be liberal in your approach to life and can be accepting of other people's individuality and ambitions. Sometimes you may have a yearning to be selfish, and just please yourself for once, because you really know how to give, and enjoy it too.

66/12/3
With a Master Number 66/12/3, you have the gift of being able to put others in the picture, particularly when they are feeling alienated or stuck out in the cold. You may enjoy listening to people's problems or even looking after your local community, or your family's needs. Loving, affectionate, and warm, you may also be emotional at times, particularly when you encounter suffering in the world.

RIGHT Trusting in your own creative talents, highlighted in Master Number 99/18/9, helps to inspire the same confidence in others.

77/14/5
With a 77/14/5 Master Number, you may be a master materializer with a gift for organization, and an ability to achieve tangible results. You may be knowledgeable, perceptive, and intuitive, and these gifts can help you to help others in life. Sometimes you may feel too bogged

FAR RIGHT With a Master Number 88/16/7, people look to you for inspiration and guidance.

THE SIGNIFICANCE OF YOUR AGE

✦ ✦ ✦ ✦ ✦ ✦ ✦ ✦ ✦ ✦ ✦ ✦ ✦ ✦ ✦ ✦ ✦ ✦

EACH YEAR IS given an age or an Age Number. Each age in your life adds up to a number between 1 to 9; for example, age 14 = 5, age 27 = 9, and so on. As you go through each stage – childhood, teenage years, adulthood, maturity – you may identify with some of the collective issues associated with each particular age. For example, when you are in your teenage years you may experience issues associated with your identity, and when you are in your 40s you may go through a 'midlife crisis'.

Sometimes it is helpful to step out of collective conditioning and view why you feel and act in particular ways during certain cycles, so that you can really be yourself during each age you experience. Of course, you will bring your own situations and circumstances to each cycle, so you always approach them with your own individuality to some extent. Each Age Number brings different experiences (along with the influences from your Personal Year Number). These pages highlight certain qualities, strengths, and challenges associated

BELOW Cast your mind back to a Personal Year Cycle to see how it's influencing you now.

with each age of your life, collectively and individually. This can help you to identify with some of the numerological information contained within each age group. However they are generalizations and account for only a few ways in which each of the numbers may influence you.

YOUR FIRST 9-YEAR CYCLE

0–9 This is collectively a time of learning and forming the psychological patterns of behavior. Individually, from your day of birth you are also forming your Personality (numerologically, your Personality Number is the day of the month in which you were born). The numbers 1 to 9 are condensed and are the most powerful numbers because they form the foundations of your life. During the ages of 1 to 4 you are learning to structure your life, to find your own rhythm and routine. Around the 5th year a deeper spiritual level influences you, and this can be a

turning point. Indeed, many children start school around this age, and it can seem traumatic. The age of 6 completes your physical cycles of experience, and from 7 to 9 you re-evaluate and integrate the lessons learned to date. Positive experiences and crisis points during this 9-year cycle may also result from the lessons of a previous life.

YOUR SECOND 9-YEAR CYCLE

9–18 Between the ages of 9 to 18 are the teenage years, when you may be learning to find your own identity and a way to express yourself as an individual. Collectively, teenage years are associated with turbulence as you work through the growing pains of developing into a young adult. As this is your second 9-year cycle, you may be asked to learn to take responsibility for yourself because you have formed your own foundations during your first 9 years. However, particularly during the age of 18, there is generally a need for experimentation and a need to learn to stand on your own two feet, highlighted in the number 18/9. This number also brings in the influence of individuality, independence, and discrimination, and with the 9 it is a time for transformation, too. This may be why 18 is generally the age of consent, when the collective deems that you are ready to be an adult. All the numbers in your teens contain a number 1, which also highlights selfishness and stubbornness as traits.

YOUR THIRD 9-YEAR CYCLE

18–27 During your early 20s you are learning to relate to life and may be collectively expected to start looking for your partner or your mate. The 2s may highlight a need to search for the other and symbolically feel complete. Individually you may feel complete on your own, but the 2 energy highlights the need to share your life with others, or even with someone who is particularly special or close to you at this time in your life. You have come through your teens, forming your own identity on your own and being selfish to some extent, so during your 20s you may feel good about having a special person or close friends with whom to share things. During this cycle you may collectively be expected to leave the nest, and perhaps to become a parent too. The number 20/2 highlights female energies (everyone has male and female energies within them), which may bring out your desire to nurture and care for others.

LEFT Infancy is the time when we absorb the psychological patterns of behavior that will influence not only this first, but all consecutive 9-year cycles.

BELOW With the first cycle over, you may learn to articulate your own opinions more clearly.

ABOVE During your fourth 9-year cycle, you may feel relaxed and happy with yourself.

RIGHT Your fifth 9-year cycle may induce you to re-evaluate your situation, perhaps to the extent of recognizing the need for new surroundings.

YOUR FOURTH 9-YEAR CYCLE

27–36 During this fourth 9-year period you may be expected to know what it is you are meant to do with your life, your career, health, and in your relationships. Numerologically this may be because the 20s highlight balance and the 30s expansion, and you may generally feel balanced and able to expand your life when you feel settled within yourself. Sometimes during the age of 27/9 you may find that you undergo deeper changes because this number highlights a connection with your inner self and your spiritual connection to others. This can be a crisis point for some, as you may consider a whole new perspective about life. Indeed, at this age you may get your first glimpse of the bigger picture as you leave behind the early adult years when personal satisfaction might have been your sole preoccupation.

YOUR FIFTH 9-YEAR CYCLE

36–45 In numerology 5 is the number for change, which is why during this cycle you may be looking backward and forward on your life, and may not know which way to go. Crisis at this stage, particularly around the age of 40, may occur if you feel stuck in the middle and lose your direction. It is a time when old values may be breaking down and new ones reforming and there may be much restlessness and impatience with the process. The 40s also influence the consolidation of your life to date, and a need to lay down foundations for the future. Many people may feel this 4 energy by wanting to re-structure their lives in some way. During your 40s you may be expected to be materially secure because the 4 highlights responsibility and material survival, but the number 5 in your cycle may shake you up with its movement.

YOUR SIXTH 9-YEAR CYCLE

45–54 During this sixth cycle, which may collectively highlight family responsibilities in your life, you may be more open to caring and looking after others, or pay more attention to your group's needs and take a bigger perspective on matters. Indeed, as an individual you are more likely to see the whole picture more clearly. The age numbers 45/9 and 54/9 influence the need to discriminate about facts, and indeed after five previous 9-year cycles you will have learned many lessons. Perhaps you find that you think things through more thoroughly before making

THE SIGNIFICANCE OF YOUR AGE

decisions, or think twice about judging others. Indeed as you move toward the ages of 49 and 50 and through to age 54 you may find that life feels fresh and full of optimism, as you have survived and are ready for some movement.

YOUR SEVENTH 9-YEAR CYCLE

54–63 During this seventh cycle you may bear the fruits of your previous 9-year cycles in terms of wisdom, finances, and experience. Indeed, collectively this period is seen as a time of maturity and relaxation. Many people retire from work around the age of 60. All this potential is contained within the 6 energy. However, at the end of the 50s you may be spending more time developing your mind. Sometimes crises arise to keep you on your toes and free up old patterns of behavior.

YOUR EIGHTH 9-YEAR CYCLE

63–72 Collectively you may be expected to slow down in life now, but many people feel a resurgence of energy, particularly if they have found a strong purpose or new goals. Indeed, the number 8 cycle highlights karmic responsibilities that you

may become aware of or complete during this 9-year cycle. You may also feel more generous with the influence of the 6 or be more able to give to your community or to loved ones. It is also a time for you to learn to nurture yourself even more. Crises may occur if you lose a sense of proportion, because the 6 influences a heightened sensitivity to life.

YOUR NINTH 9-YEAR CYCLE

72–81 During your 70s you may be expected to become fragile; this quality is contained within the number 7. You may also feel vulnerable, or feel like protecting yourself. This may result from the 7 influence, which is asking you to go inside and connect with your inner self. Sometimes you may find that your intuition is acute and perhaps people come to you to benefit from your inner wisdom. You may not always be quiet and introspective, because in your 70s you may also be influenced by a fast-moving energy.

YOUR TENTH 9-YEAR CYCLE

81+ This is a time for rebirth, for going back to childhood in your memories. Rebirth can mean you need to adjust to a different pace in life, as it is a time to view every area of your life closely. The number 8 highlights a need to be assertive and stand on your own two feet. The 8 also influences the spiritual will that drives you forward and you may recognize the saying, "Where there's a will there's a way." You may even be so strong-willed that you become a force to be reckoned with.

LEFT Your inner wisdom may really shine through during your seventh 9-year cycle.

ABOVE Nostalgic keepsakes and photographs are powerful reminders of how your life has developed over the years.

THE FIVE SENSES

* * * * * * * * * * * * * * * * * *

A HUMAN BEING IS born with 5 senses and in numerology five is associated with soul influences. The collective soul and your individual soul can contact you through these 5 senses. You may notice that one particular sense is stronger than the others; perhaps you are needing to learn about one sense more than another. For example, if you are blind, then your hearing may be acute, so this may be a way for you to relate to the world. Perhaps you are very good at listening to people and therefore may become a professional counselor.

Indeed, each of your senses is a gift that you may take for granted; sometimes you may learn to appreciate these senses only when you are in old age, perhaps because your sense of hearing decreases or you need to wear glasses to see. Some children are also born with different senses missing, and as they grow up they may be aware of other ways in which they can relate to the world. When you die your physical body lets go of each of your senses one by one, as you move out of physical reality into another level of being or consciousness.

You may have also heard of the sixth sense, which all humans possess because humans have developed from the animal kingdom. This sixth sense is called instinct, and it is a way by which you are able to relate to people and to the world through your feelings.

When somebody close to you dies, then you may be aware of the power of your instincts, as you may get in touch with deep emotions or feelings of separation and because that person was once a part of your pack. Sometimes you may get a premonition or a gut feeling about a situation in your life. These can help to teach you many lessons, whether they are right or merely leading you into illusions.

In numerology each number highlights a specific sense that you may be particularly learning about in this lifetime. Your five senses are together teaching you to relate to life with your own unique vision of the world. This section focuses particularly on your Personality Number and the psychological trends of behaviors associated with it, but you can also look up your other major numbers which highlight ways in which you relate to these senses. You can also look up any of your compound numbers individually, as these influence you to a degree. For example, if your Life Path Number is a 41/5, then you can look up the 4 and 1 as sub-influences, along with the main number which is a 5.

HEARING (2,6)

With the numbers 2 and 6 in your chart, you are learning about the sense of hearing, and the way in which you listen (or don't listen) to what people around you are saying. Perhaps you love listening to what people have to say and are a good listener, or at times you may block people out and not want to listen to them. You may also find that when you have heard something you didn't want to hear, you stop listening to people fully and disregard what people are saying. In life, much time is wasted and confrontational situations arise because people don't listen to what is being said, or they do not hear what they are saying to others.

TOUCH (3,4)

You may be particularly aware of the sense of touch if you have the numbers 3 or 4 in your chart; you may learn to value life by how much physical connection or touch there is. With a 3 you may be very tactile and therefore generally feel loved when others hug you or hold your hand, and with a 4 you may feel more secure when people are physically near to you. Touch also helps you to feel real because it can offer physical confirmation, which is why in the bigger world at large touch is an important way of bringing people closer together. If you don't like being touched, then this may be a way of cutting off or staying separate from the world.

SIGHT (5,7)

With the numbers 5 or 7 in your chart, you may be learning particularly about the sense of sight. Like all the senses that feed you information, your sight gives you a sense of proportion by allowing you to form a picture of what life looks like, as well as providing you with visual information. Along with your other senses you then interpret the things you see to form your own view of the world. Everybody perceives things differently and this creates challenging situations in the world. However, there are also many ways in which we see things in the same way: the humanitarian term "one world vision of peace" is an example, though it may be approached and executed in many different ways by people with a different vision.

TASTE (1,5)

You may be particularly learning about the sense of taste if you have the numbers 1 or 5 in your chart. What you taste can have a powerful influence in your life. If you eat something sweet, then psychologically it may make you feel good, and if you eat something sour it may make you feel bitter or sour. Of course, eating sweet or sour foods can bring out many other different psychological reactions in you, to some extent depending on your mood. Taste may help you to value what you like and don't like about yourself and about life. Learning to appreciate other people's tastes in the bigger world at large may be what these numbers are teaching you.

SMELL (8,9)

With the numbers 8 or 9 in your chart you may particularly be learning about the sense of smell. Perhaps you have a keen sense, like a tracker dog that is able to locate its needs using this gift. Or you may have a poor sense of smell and rely more on other senses instead. Smells can uplift or repulse you or change your mood, and can bring back powerful memories from the past as you link certain smells to events psychologically associated with them. Individuals have their own smell. You

may also identify with the bigger world at large by smell; each culture has its own particular smell, and each geographical area has its own native fragrances. The earth also has its own overall smell from all the nations on this planet put together too!

INSTINCT AND INTUITION

* * * * * * * * * * * * * * * * * * *

INSTINCT AND INTUITION are two different qualities used every day. They may appear the same, but they are in effect very different, because instinct links you with your inner sense of feelings and emotional desires, and intuition links you with your inner sense of knowing and the process of the mind. Many people use both, though some use more of one aspect than the other and at different times of life.

RIGHT A hunting scene carved in stone echoes man's most basic instinct to track animals for survival.

INSTINCT

In numerology, if you have the numbers 2, 3, 6, and 9 in your chart, particularly as major numbers like your Personality or Life Path Number, then you may relate well to your instincts. This means that you are tuned into your gut feelings about things that happen to you. For example, you may be offered two new jobs, which could lead you down completely different avenues in life. You may weigh up the facts about each one, talk to your nearest and dearest about them, and spend time working out the practical pros and cons for each position, but you may simply decide to take the job that feels right, because your instincts arise from feelings deep within you. Of course your feelings may not always be right, because they may be based on desires, so you may be swayed by a lack of objectivity.

Sometimes your gut feelings can be helpful and act as guidelines, because at the very least they let you know how you feel at any moment of the day. You may also get premonitions based on your feelings, or psychic dreams that also help to give you guidance about your

RIGHT Instinct is inherent in the way we would hesitate to cross the road.

own life and other peoples. You may have very strong feelings indeed about those close to you, because as a human being your immediate family and friends are a part of your "pack."

Instincts may be really helpful when you are unable to see your way out of a situation or are confused with your life. Your instincts can also help you to survive; for example, if you are crossing a road and you see no traffic but your feelings tell you to wait, you may then avoid a fast-moving motorbike careering around the corner. Instincts remain from the times of cave dwellers when we needed this sense in order to survive. Instincts also play a large part of our collective conditioning. Many people in the world collective may want to own a television or a car, and such collective desires can make you feel the odd one out if you don't want the same things as the masses. The earth is a watery planet, and your physical body is mainly made up of water too, which is why emotions, which are associated with water, have such a pull over you. This is particularly the case if you have 2, 3, 6, and 9 in your chart as major numbers.

Importantly your instincts draw you to choose certain people in life, particularly physically, and these instincts can be difficult to avoid. You may not like a person, such as an ex-partner, but the instinctual physical or sexual attraction may be still strong.

INTUITION

Everyone has the ability to connect with intuition; some people do it sub-consciously and others may consciously tune in to their higher self or to the knowledge which comes through their mind via their soul. You may find that you are more aware or sensitive to your intuition if you have the numbers 1, 5, 7, or 8 in your chart, particularly as major numbers.

Intuition can be described as moments of revelation. For example, you may have been working your way through a project at work and have reached a deadlock. Your instincts or feelings may be telling you two different things as you waver back and forth, undecided, but the answer to your problem may suddenly come in a flash of inspiration. Indeed, one of the differences between instinct and intuition is that instinct is associated with the emotions, while intuition is associated with the mind. Indeed, no emotion is attached to intuition. It is something that seems matter-of-fact, so you may wonder why you didn't think of your inspired idea in the first place.

You may also have intuitive dreams which are different from psychic dreams, as you usually feel indiffer-ence with an intuitive dream and deep feel-ings in a psychic or instinctual dream. Dreams flowing from your intuition may seem so crystal clear that you can't possi-bly get emotional about them. They may also seem still, and very real.

Intuition can also be mixed up with your mental thoughts, particularly if you have an active intellect. Everyone thinks what they want most of the time, but intuition may speak to give you guid-ance about things you couldn't possibly imagine even if you tried.

Intuition is also used to help others because it is linked to your soul. It rarely pops up simply to guide you, even if it may seem like that at the time. For example, if your intuition is telling you that you need to move from the company you work for, it may be for the best for the whole family. Perhaps being in a job that is satisfying means that you feel happier within yourself and with your whole family. Intuition is therefore a factor which connects you and can bring you closer to others. Responsibility is the key lesson for everyone on earth. Whether you work with your emotions and instincts or with your mind and your intuition is irrelevant because this lesson remains the same. It is only by taking responsibility for yourself that you can make the most out of life.

LEFT A businessman's intuition may present solutions where he may have previously been indecisive.

9

BELOW Intuitive dreams present themselves as real.

MIND, BODY, AND SPIRIT

★★★★★★★★★★★★★★★★★★

MANY PEOPLE now recognize that there is more to life than simply the physical level of existence. The term "holistic" is a word that implies the whole of the mind, body, and spirit, and it is often referred to in complementary therapy, because practitioners take a view of the "whole" of their patients' health, instead of treating isolated symptoms. "Mind, body, and spirit" also refers to the inter-connected-ness of life, which can be identified in the numerological cycles.

RIGHT As the mind, body, and spirit are interconnected, choosing to embark on a physical journey may speak volumes about yourself.

MIND

In numerology the numbers 1, 5, or 8 are associated with the mind, which is strongly linked to the soul. Your soul communicates to you through your mind, and when it does so you may feel a sense of clarity. Sometimes your mind produces thoughts that are not from your soul, but which are an interpretation of your own mental projection. The more open and receptive your mind, the better you can communicate with your soul and express this energy to others. Your soul is your connection to a part of you which continues after your

BELOW Complementary practitioners understand the need to identify with the patient's health as a whole.

death, and your connection with the group soul of all the people living in the world today.

Sometimes it is your soul that provides your direction in life. This subtle energy guides you in the best possible direction for the lessons you need to learn. In numerology your Soul Number gives you clues about the way in which this energy influences you. Your Life Path Number also contains elements of soul, and all life on earth today is as a result of the impulse of soul life.

When you try to inhibit soul energy, perhaps by staying centered in your personal desires, then your physical energy may slow down. It is said that all illness and disease in the world today occurs as a result of an inhibited soul life. Your soul has needs, which may be very different from your own personal desires. For example, your soul may influence you to work with the underprivileged, or to help a friend but your ego may not want to do so.

The soul also introduces a sense of joy, which is different from happiness, because joy is a state of beingness and not an emotion; joy is found by connecting with your soul. Your soul energy also weaves its way through your life and highlights your individuality.

BODY

You may be particularly concerned with your body if you have the numbers 3, 4, or 6 in your chart. This is because the 4 is an earthly energy that preoccupies itself with material issues (and so does the 8, to some degree). The 3 energy means that you may usually be very active in the physical world and the number 6 highlights emotional security, which may seem of equal or of more importance to your physical survival. You may be a physical person who enjoys touching, hugs, cuddles, and making love. You may feel particularly concerned with issues concerning your physical body. Sometimes your body may seem cumbersome, as if it gets in the way; for example, you may wish you could walk faster, be more robust, or even be more physically sensitive.

Sometimes, when you focus only on the material side of life, other areas of life become off-balance. For example, with some health problems, all the money in the world may not be able to help you recover. However, you may sometimes be so busy running around in the world that you have no time to stop and listen, whereupon illness forces you to pay your soul full attention.

SPIRIT

Everyone is spiritual because everyone and everything is ultimately connected, whether or not you feel it, because you share the same world and the same universe. You are more likely to be aware of your spirituality if you have the numbers 2, 7, or 9 in your chart. This is because the number 2 reflects an openness and a receptivity to all areas of life,

including the spiritual elements. The 7 influences introspection and a need to go inside and connect with your inner spiritual guidance, in order to materialize these aspects. With a 9 you may be adaptable and broad-minded in your outlook on life, so you may readily encompass spirituality as an ordinary part of life.

Spirituality is not special; it simply is. When you think of spirituality you may think of a specific religion, or of people carrying out good deeds, but even when people do or say things you may judge to be wrong they are still being spiritual in another way, because they are learning through their experience of life. In order to understand goodness you also need to be able to contact your shadow or inner self, to bring in the spiritual energies that can transform those elements into light. This may be done through simple awareness. Spirituality, therefore, is about being true to yourself and having the integrity to be your own person, no matter what other people say or do to convince you otherwise. Following your own inner connection to your spirituality can help you grow, both in your relationships with other people, your relationship with yourself, and your attitude to the world.

Spirituality also highlights the collective need for good will and healthy human relations, so that the whole of humanity is able to live in peace together and discover a sense of harmony within itself.

THE ELEMENTS

* * * * * * * * * * * * * * * * * *

TRADITIONALLY in the West people see everything in the world as being made up from four elements: earth, air, fire, and water, but in the East there is often an additional fifth category, metal. In numerology 4 is the number that highlights planet Earth and 5 is associated with the soul. In the East these elements are regarded as very auspicious and people pay great attention to their potential influence. For example, they may change their living environments to align with the specific element influencing each year, perhaps by introducing more water or wood features into their homes, while removing certain other less favorable elements. The year 2000 in numerology adds up to a 2, which highlights the element of water or the emotions, and this element will influence the whole of the next millennium.

RIGHT *"Forced Combustion."* When pressure builds up, it is released into the air. Volcanoes are examples of this.

All these elements can be seen influencing you and working their way into your life from the numbers in your chart. You have many numbers in your chart, but the digits that each major number adds up to give you clues, so you may have a 9 Personality Number which is fiery, or a 7 Life Path Number which is watery. When looking at all the major numbers in your chart one or two numbers may be predominant, or you may have a mixture of all of them. Look up information for each of your major numbers to see the significance of each number in your life, so that you can see how each element relates to you. For example, your Personality Number relates to psychological patterns of behavior, so if this number is a 9 you may be more passionate or fiery at times (and, at the other extreme, very laid-back when the fire falls dormant).

Each of the elements in your chart also determines your physical traits, as your body is but a mirror of the energy influencing you. Indeed you may have noticed that the shape of your face changes when you are going through great transformations in your life, such as getting married, having a child, or experiencing a trauma of some kind; everyone has their life experiences etched on their faces. The qualities contained within your potential are being brought out and used strongly, mirroring them externally. If you observe your Personal Year Number, it can help you to see why certain situations occur during specific times of your life. For example, you may have a predominantly earthy chart, so when you are in a fire year this may change your physical appearance. The extent to which you are affected depends upon how much you are working with the energies contained within their potential.

It is also interesting to look at yourself and those around you to see the numbers predominant in their lives at different times. For example, if you have a 3 Personality Number and an 8 Life Path Number, then you may physically look more a fiery 3 (muscular) when you are young and more earthy (solid) when you are older. All of the numbers in your chart are moving and fluctuating energies that you can read from your body.

LEFT The element of earth has a stabilizing influence in our lives.

EARTH

If you have the numbers 4 and 8 in your chart, then you have the element of earth influencing you to some degree. Therefore you may be down-to-earth, practical, efficient, and hard-working, approaching life in a step-by-step manner. However, you may feel insecure at times, and you may be preoccupied with the material side of existence. Money may also be an issue with an earthy number influencing your life.

Physically, you may have a rough or sallow complexion, dark skin, coarse hair, heavy eyelids, wide cheekbones, a strong jaw, but a long, oblong face. You may also have a lisp or even stutter or an alluring and deep voice.

FIRE

If one of the major numbers in your chart is a 3 or 9, then you may have the element of fire influencing you. This highlights passion and a fiery temperament that often blows hot and cold. However, with the 3 and 9 influencing you, you may also have an adaptable view on life, so the fire may remain under control. All the same, your fearsome temper may rear up unexpectedly at times, and surprise people who assumed you were easygoing. You may be social, humorous, lighthearted, and at other times intense, and you may particularly enjoy conversation and discussion.

Physically you may have a very lean and muscular body, with strong hips. You may look sporty or rugged. You may have a square face, a long neck, and bright eyes, and you may have a bulbous nose.

AIR

The numbers 1 and 5 highlight the element of air in your chart, particularly if these are major numbers. You may be wilful, focused, and ambitious, possessing a head full of ideas, some of which can linger for too long. Stimulation and communication may be important, and you may have a strong sense of fun and adventure.

Physically you may have prominent or high cheekbones, a high forehead, large bulging eyes, a long neck, thin lips, a serious tone of voice, and a tall and slim body with long legs and narrow hips.

ABOVE Air symbolizes the winds of change that bring fresh opportunities for growth.

WATER

With the numbers 2, 6, and 7 in your chart you are influenced by the element of water. You may be sensitive and intuitive and also possess a strong instinct. You may feel open to the world, and at times too vulnerable. You can be gentle, patient, and enjoy sharing your life. You may also sometimes wallow in your feelings or even cut off from your emotions.

Physically you may have a round or heart-shaped face, watery and sensitive eyes, a delicate skin tone, a straight nose, and full lips. Your overall appearance may look rounded and fleshy. You may sometimes possess a whispery or gentle voice and at other times it may have a sharp tone.

LEFT Fire embodies a natural zeal for life, raw energy, and assertiveness.

BELOW Water influences the ebb and flow of emotional currents.

MANDALAS

★ ★ ★ ★ ★ ★ ★ ★ ★ ★ ★ ★ ★ ★ ★

A MANDALA IS A drawing or figure used to help you connect with your inner self and to other dimensions in the universe. It is traditionally an 8-sided figure with the 9th position being its center. As 8 is a number that represents karma, you can see why the whole of life may appear to be contained within this digit. A mandala is said to be able to give you information about the past (or past lives), the present, and the future. In numerology each of its elements represents its position in the cycle of 1 to 9.

Mandalas have been used for thousands of years by many people around the world. They are still popular today. The Tibetan Buddhists sometimes travel to the West to show their skills at making the most intricate mandalas out of sand. They have been known to spend days making one mandala, with perhaps up to four monks working on the same masterpiece. Once perfected, it is then destroyed, and they start again. This represents the impermanance of life, which is always changing: life, death, and rebirth become one. Many ancient religions made mandalas as offerings to their gods; some of these were also three-dimensional.

DRAWING YOUR MANDALA WITH NUMEROLOGY

Mandalas are useful "mirrors" to reflect your inner self, and can be used as a tool in introspection, meditation, or thought as you focus on making your own wonderful creations. They can also teach you about the bigger picture in life. You can make mandalas out of fabric or sand, or simply draw them with pencils, crayons, or colored felt-tip pens. If you feel more artistic you can paint them with acrylics on canvas.

Numerology is your own personal signature tune. By applying the numbers from your chart into your own mandala it can help to give you more information about your life. For example, you can see numbers, colors, and shapes all together in your own mandala, which may give you a different perspective on life, and can maybe help you change the way you are living it. Perhaps you may like to meditate by spending time looking into your mandala, or simply by visualizing it in your mind. Here are some processes which you may like to carry out with numbers and mandalas. Be creative, and have fun.

ABOVE A fun complement to charting your numbers is to create your own colorful mandala.

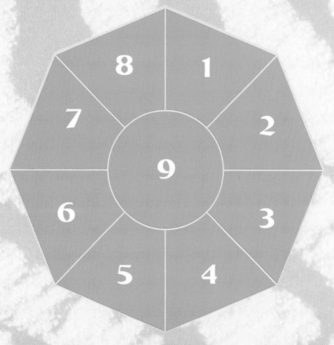

LEFT An example
of a Life Mandala
for Personality
Number 17/8.

MAKING THE TEMPLATE
OF A MANDALA

Draw an 8-sided figure and in the center place a circle. Each of the segments represents numbers 1 to 8, with 9 in the center. In numerology number 9 contains all the numbers 1 to 8 within its potential (see the illustration). You can now draw what you wish in the mandala, using the following ideas for inspiration. You may also find that you enter a meditative level of consciousness while you are constructing your mandalas.

Your Life Mandala

Your date of birth carries two of the most significant numbers in your chart; your Personality and Life Path Numbers. You may like to shade these two numbers in your mandala in colors, or you may like to draw illustrations within them. For example, if you were born on March 17, 1986 then you may draw in the full 17/8 (the day in the month) and 44/8 (the whole date of birth), see the illustration above.

Every digit in your date of birth influences your life and is potent, so you may draw your whole date of birth or other illustrations within these areas (see the illustration). It may be a very powerful experience to look at this whole date of birth in your own mandala. Perhaps you may like to keep it up on a wall or somewhere you can see it on a daily basis. Each time you look at your mandala you bring a different perspective and look at it in a different light because you are constantly changing. It is therefore a powerful teaching tool.

ABOVE Your date
of birth is
important when
drawing up your
Life Mandala.

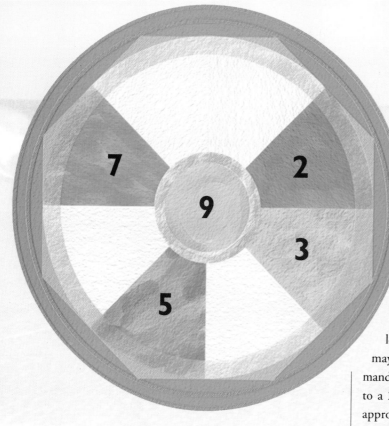

Individual Name Mandalas

Your first name or Goal Number influences some of the major goals set for you to learn in life. Because everyone calls you by this name, its numerological influences are strong. Your last name or Family Name, which you were born with, highlights the group karma or lessons which you are learning with your family. Any middle names bring additional qualities, strengths, and challenges which may influence your life. You may like to place each name onto a separate mandala. For example, the name Mary adds up to a 21/3, so you may like to shade in these appropriate areas or you may like to draw in illustrations in these areas.

ABOVE Personal Year and Age Mandala for Age Number 27/9 and Personal Year Number 32/5.

Your Past Life Mandala

Your Soul Number and your Karma Number give information about past lives or lessons you may be needing to learn in this lifetime. Your soul is always guiding you, even though you may not be conscious of its presence. If your Soul Number is a 69/15/6 and your Karma Number is a 71/8, then you may like to shade in all the areas that correspond with these digits in your Mandala. You may also like to draw illustrations in these areas. Before you draw this mandala you may like to take a little time to meditate beforehand so that you can approach it with an open mind.

RIGHT Past Life Mandala for Soul Number 69/15/6 and Karma Number 71/8.

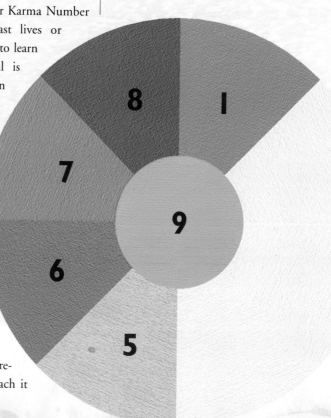

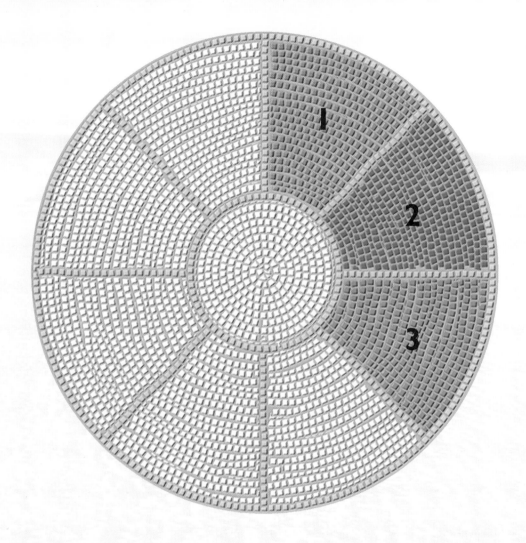

Personal Year And Age Mandala

You may like to draw a mandala for the Personal Year Number which is currently influencing you, and incorporate into it your Age Number. For example, you may be aged 27, so your Age Number is 27/9, and your Personal Year Number may be a 32/5. In that case you can shade in all these numbers in their appropriate areas, or draw your own illustrations in these areas. This may help to mirror to you the energies that are particularly influencing you at this time.

Important Or Memorable Dates

Important dates such as your wedding day, a birthday, or·the date you passed your driving test, can all be included on a mandala, which may help you to learn what these situations may have been teaching you. For example, if you set up your own business and the first day of trading was July 31, 1998, then you can shade in all these digits on your mandala or again draw in illustrations within them.

Comparison Mandalas

A mandala may be a useful tool to highlight your potential within your personal relationships. By shading in the Personality, Life Path, Soul, Childhood, or Karma Numbers of both of you together, you may gain information about how your energies blend together on these different levels. (See Comparing Numbers for more information, pages 104–9).

BELOW Tibetan buddhists create the most detailed and colorful mandalas from sand.

ASTROLOGY

* * * * * * * * * * * * * * * * * * *

ABOVE The zodiac is divided into twelve sections, each with its own name and symbol.

ASTROLOGY IS AN ancient method of finding out more about life and the energies that influence you, based on the date and time of your birth in relation to planetary configurations. It is the unique line-up of planets at the exact time you were born that gives you your Personality characteristics, your potential in life, and potential times for events to occur in your life.

There are 12 astrological signs. They also influence world events and situations that humanity is working through collectively. These planetary positions are constantly changing and forging a unique relationship with each other at any moment in time. The name of each planet can be added up numerologically to provide information about what it is helping to teach you, and each planetary configuration is influenced by numbers as the planets align at specific times and dates.

Your birth sign is shared by one-twelfth of the world's population and at any time millions of people are all influenced by the same energies, although you may be working through these lessons in very different personal ways. As you enter each month you are also influenced by each month's energies, but these may become more potent if that specific month is your month of birth. This means that the qualities or lessons it may be teaching you are intensified during this time. If you were born in July, then every July (month 7) you may experience a mini rebirth and aspects of your life may come flooding back, while your energies are also renewing themselves in order to begin a new 12-month cycle. One of the qualities of the 7 is trust, and during this time situations may arise involving this issue.

Find your birth sign below and learn a little more about how it may be influencing your life. Each sign falls across two different months and, like numbers that flow through each other, each month flows into the next. If you were born in July, for example, under the sign of Cancer, you may also be influenced to a lesser degree by the qualities of the signs before and after, which are Gemini and Leo. Aries is traditionally seen as the first sign of the zodiac because it occurs at the spring equinox, but Capricorn falls in the first month and hence is given the number 1 in numerology.

ABOVE A celestial globe depicting the stars and constellations.

Capricorn = 1 Number 1 highlights inspiration, leadership, new direction, focus, ambition and the relentless determination of the spiritual warrior. Challenges may include: carelessness, selfishness, and self-motivation. One major lesson associated with the number 1 may be that of discovering how to be fully independent, so that you can look after your personal needs in life.

90

Aquarius = 2 Number 2 highlights sharing, a need to relate to others through feelings and emotions, diplomacy, and co-operation. Challenges may include hypersensitivity, defensiveness, and confrontation. One major lesson associated with this number 2 may be the need to learn to be receptive to life, so that you can open up to what it has to offer, and perhaps be able to give more.

Pisces = 3 Number 3 influences joy and laughter, activity, sponteneity creativity, adaptability, freedom and the ability to communicate. Challenges may include criticism, confusion, a feeling of unease and cynicism. A major lesson associated with the number 3 may be that of furthering the development of the skill of relating to people in all kinds of different social situations. This may also help you to enhance your confidence in life.

ABOVE These are the numbers that relate to each astrological symbol.

Aries = 4 Number 4 highlights structure, discipline, boundaries, loyalty, security, and determination. Challenges may include complacency, resistance to change, a tendency to struggle, and melancholia. Major lessons associated with this number 4 may be learning to take responsibility for yourself and your actions and to allow yourself to feel more passionate about life.

Taurus = 5 Number 5 influences movement, self-expression, magnetism, adventure, commitment, and versatility. Challenges may include fluctuation, restriction, scepticism, and insistence. A major lesson associated with this number 5 may be in allowing life to be your teacher by allowing it to show you your next step, rather than trying to dominate the process of change yourself.

Gemini = 6 Number 6 influences love, compassion, caring, generosity, and devotion. Challenges may include jealousy, self-pity, resentment, and envy. A major lesson associated with this number 6 may be that of learning to open up your heart to life and all its experiences, and finding love for those who may appear to you to be undeserving of it, as well as for those who you think might be worthy of it and reasonably expect it.

Cancer = 7 Number 7 influences productivity, emotional sensitivity, solitude, intuition, and purity. Challenges may include isolation, vulnerability, vagueness, and inferiority. One of the major lessons associated with the number 7 may be that of learning to find your own truth in any situation, as a part of your own personal development, rather than accepting received opinions or the judgements of others.

ABOVE Astrology and numerology work together to reveal the major influences and potential in each person's life.

Leo = 8 Number 8 influences karma, power, passion, charm, organization, and strength. Challenges may include bullying, abuse, rigidity, and vanity. One of the major lessons of this number 8 may be that of learning to find your own inner strength so that you do not feel that you always have to fight life, but can stand up to things by simply being yourself.

Virgo = 9 Number 9 influences leadership, humor, compassion, selflessness, and inspiration. Challenges may include rebelliousness, humiliation, self-importance, and laziness. One of the major lessons of the number 9 may be to drop unrealistic high expectations, and learn to accept life as it is.

Libra = 10/1 Number 10/1 influences wisdom, knowledge, understanding, ambition and focus. Challenges may include defeat, loss of purpose, a weak will, and ignorance. One of the major lessons of the number 10/1 may be

to work on the development of your inner knowledge to help direct others in life in the best possible way. You may also find that this gives you direction in your life path too, and helps you with your relationships with yourself and others.

Scorpio = 11/2 Number 11/2 influences inspiration, motivation, spiritual will, magnetism, and co-operation. Challenges may include fear, emotional instability, and indecision. One of the major lessons of the number 11/2 may be that of learning how to lead others without the need to prove yourself or your self-worth. You may constantly feel the need to express your individuality or impress your personality on others.

Sagittarius = 12/3 Number 12/3 influences logic, flexibility, self-expression, love, and beauty. Challenges may include intrusion, isolation, and criticism. One of the major lessons of the 12/3 may be that of learning to use your intuition and instincts to help guide you.

BELOW People express some positive and negative traits that correspond to a particular planetary or numerical energy.

TAROT

* * * * * * * * * * * * * * * *

THE TAROT IS A METHOD of understanding more about yourself and life by looking at cards that each depict symbols which represent some aspect of life. Each card has a corresponding number, which offers numerological information about what it represents. In a set of Tarot cards there are generally 78 cards, with 22 cards representing the Major Arcana and 56 representing the Minor Arcana.

In numerology 78 adds up to 15/6; the whole number represents the use of the mind, the intuition, and the instincts. The number 15/6 also represents wholeness or the whole of life, completion, and a need to see the overall picture or obtain a larger one. The 8 influences karma and the wheel of fortune or fate as it spins its destiny. The 22 of the Major Arcana symbolize the important bigger issues or lessons in life. In numerology 22 is the building block of life which sets firm foundations for others to work upon, with its vision of group goals to materialize, and the challenge to do this in a responsible way. The 56 Minor Arcana cards are associated with everyday situations and this number adds up to an 11/2, which influences the ability to uplift people with spiritual energies and create a unity or connection to the whole of humanity. Again, it is asking you to relate to the overall picture.

The Tarot is an ancient system which many people use for prediction to give them black and white answers to questions on the physical level. For example, you may shuffle the deck of cards, and then ask the question, "Will I get a new car next week?" The card number 1, the Magician, may be conjured up, which you may feel is telling you that you will. These symbols may also be interpreted on the emotional, mental, and spiritual levels too. For example,

ABOVE, RIGHT, AND FAR RIGHT A popular form of divination, Tarot is a tool for exploring the subconscious, highlighting possible choices and routes we may pursue.

your emotional desire to buy a new car may not mean that you follow through on the physical action of buying it. Life is only one part physical reality and there are three other areas to relate to life.

Work out your Personality, Life Path, Soul, Childhood, and Karma Numbers, along with your Personal Year Number, and look them up in the list of 22 Major Arcana Symbols and Numbers below to give you some general trends associated with them, which may also influence your life.

0: The Fool Zero contains the full potential of all life. Perhaps you may misuse your potential or take it for granted.

1: Magician The mind helps to think up the concepts and the will helps to materialize them into reality, but in life nothing is 100 percent certain.

2: High Priestess Wisdom and knowledge are represented through experience. Your intuition may guide you, but your emotions may lead you astray.

3: Empress Joy is a gift that can be demonstrated to others but not shared like laughter, because joy comes from within.

4: Emperor The path to wisdom and knowledge is gained by experience. Any resistance to life may be a latent fear that you have of living your life fully in the present.

5: Heirophant Being able to appreciate the many different delicacies in life, which are all a part of the whole, may enable you to teach others this lesson.

6: Lovers Life grows out of the zero of potential and the 1 of the spiritual will to make it happen, and love may blossom.

7: Chariot Nature has the power to build and to destroy as it breaks through with its lessons and you learn to become self-conscious.

8: Strength The greatest strength is found in vulnerability. Letting life flow takes little effort, but opposing the flow is exhausting.

9: Hermit Solitude may be needed in order to explore the depths of your mind. Human contact and humor may allow you to touch others with your spirituality.

10/1: Wheel Of Fortune Rebirth gives you more time to learn essential lessons, and to set your goals ahead.

11/2: Justice You have the power to measure and weigh up what you think is needed and what feels right or best for you and whoever else is concerned.

12/3: Hanged Man Confusion and resistance are usually what happens before important changes. But life takes you forward anyway, and you can do nothing to stop it.

13/4: Death Transformation is a natural part of life. Heaven and Earth are both needed in the balancing act.

14/5: Temperance Life serves you well with the lessons you need to learn; by releasing any self-imposed restrictions you are free to learn.

15/6: Devil Separation may describe evil or the devil, but its other polarity is goodness and connection; both are parts of nature.

16/7: Tower There is no shelter from life, truth has nowhere (or no need) to hide. Your inner light illuminates the truth in others' lives.

17/8: Star Life bursts with energy like stars that radiate into the night, revealing the information you need.

18/9: Moon The moon is the great nurturer that provides energy to help you open up to your intuition.

19/1: Sun The burning rays of the sun help to purify your mind and your emotions to let you move forward with new understanding.

20/2: Judgement Any decision you make can teach you more about life; using your instincts and your logical brain may help guide you toward the right decision.

21/3: World The world prospers even though poverty exists; spirituality unites the world for richer or for poorer, in sickness and in health.

RELATIONSHIPS

★ ★ ★ ★ ★ ★ ★ ★ ★ ★ ★ ★ ★ ★ ★ ★ ★ ★

RELATIONSHIPS MAKE THE world go around. When you consider relationships, you may instantly think of people – lovers, partners, family, friends, children. But you have a relationship to everything – the moon, the stars, the earth, the sun, and air; the list is endless. You also have a relationship with food, for example, as well as the bigger things in life.

How you will relate to life – your relationships – is highlighted in the numbers in your chart. Each of the numbers in your chart also have a relationship to one another and this unique flow of energy guides you through life. The numbers or cycles in your chart are moving energies, flowing through each other consecutively. For example, if you have a 9 Life Path Number, then the preceding and following numbers, 8 and 1, will also be influencing you to some extent. In numerology, numbers can be seen upside down, inside out, back to front, and in whatever way your wisdom guides you to receive more information. Each cycle or number can help you learn the lessons and offers strengths and challenges contained within their potential. The challenging or "negative" aspects of your chart are often the most useful because they can teach you so much about yourself. Only by knowing and loving yourself, it is said, can you truly love others. This includes your inner spiritual self along with the physical, emotional, and mental levels of your being. Consult the major numbers in your chart here, simultaneously allowing your inner wisdom and intuition to help you see the overall picture of how you relate to the significant people in your life.

BELOW Life comprises of interwoven energies, and these influence our unique relationships with other people.

CHILDREN

1 Children with a 1 may need great care and attention because they may be withdrawn and sensitive and need bringing out of themselves to develop in life. They may enjoy showing off their talents and gifts to their friends. These children need to be encouraged to find their own individuality, and in their relationships with others they may often want to take the lead.

2 Children with a 2 are forming relationships in life that can teach them to get along and to co-operate with others. They may relish affection, but they may push people away if they try to get too close, particularly emotionally. Occasionally they may seem secretive about their feelings, while at other times they may laugh, cry, and express their feelings, no matter who is around.

3 These children love to play, but may be really naughty at times and be always getting up to mischief. In relationships they may tend to attract friends who can withstand the rough and tumble of everyday life with them, and may need to be stimulated by lots of different friends and people around them. In their relationships they may be effusive.

4 Children with a 4 may like to have friends come and play with them at their homes, as they usually need a base to help them feel secure. They may stick to the same friends throughout childhood, which helps to regulate their daily routine. These children may be very physical and enjoy hugs and holding hands; again, it often helps them to feel secure.

5 These children may enjoy spontaneity, but let others down because they are so changeable. They may still be popular because they can bring fun and adventure into others' lives. These children may love to have plenty of freedom, while at the same time need discipline to show them where the boundaries lie. They may like friends who are alert and can teach them more about life.

6 Children with a 6 may enjoy being a part of a group of friends and like to feel that they belong. In their relationships they may be warm and caring and look after their friends and those around them. They may also love to look after animals too, which gives them a sense of responsibility and helps them to open their heart to life. At times they may become deeply emotionally attached to friends or loved ones.

LEFT The expression of loyalty in friendships is important to a child with a 4.

ABOVE Having a competitive streak; children with an 8.

LEFT Happiest when absorbed in play, children with a 3 also demand an audience.

RIGHT Number 1;
as a parent you
may inspire your
child with regular
one-to-one activity.

BELOW Number 2;
you may dedicate
your life to family
matters.

7 Children with a 7 may be very honest and open and like friends who can be honest too. Indeed, these children tend to be blunt at times, and seem harsh because of their direct honesty. Sometimes this does not always endear them to others. In their relationships these children need to be understood, so that they do not feel like they are wrong, but are simply being themselves.

8 These children may enjoy competition and may like to be in relationships with friends who can compete with them so that it urges them to try harder. At times, paradoxically, they may only lead or take part when they think they know they are going to win. In their relationships these children may need to learn to stand up for themselves, though they may sometimes be very bossy.

9 Children with a 9 often enjoy taking command. Indeed, they may tend to attract friends who need direction. In their relationships they may admire certain qualities in others openly, and aspire to be acceptable so that they can fit in. They may work hard to gain others' approval.

PARENTS

1 As parents you may like to lead your children and give them direction with their lives, although you may not always find this easy. Sometimes it may seem that your children are your direction in life and that they are guiding you. Intimacy may be a challenge and you may prefer to keep your children at arm's length, and you may encourage your child to be independent from an early age.

2 As a parent with a 2 you may enjoy giving and receiving love with your children. You may feel the emotional bonds with your children strongly and when they grow up you may feel their emotions intensely, too. You may teach your children to open their hearts to life and to relate to people emotionally. Children may help to bring out your wisdom.

3 With a 3, you may enjoy bringing joy into your children's lives by teaching them to play and enjoy the fun side of life. However, you may not give them all the attention they need, although you may be easily distracted by your child at times. Generally, you can be very giving. You may be able to teach your children to feel free to express themselves in life.

4 As a parent with a 4, you may give your children a solid home base so that they feel comfortable with life. One of the ways you may do this is by encouraging them to take responsibility for themselves, and to show them that you are a responsible parent too. You may enjoy relating physically to your children, perhaps by joining in with sports, or outdoor activities, possibly as a part of a regular routine.

5 With a 5, you may like to encourage children to ask questions so that you can share your knowledge. You may show them how to look for the facts in any situation; perhaps you may be sceptical, which helps teach them to work things out for themselves. You may be a magnetic person and therefore teach your child to enjoy being with people.

6 With a 6, you may be showing your children that you are a dutiful parent so that they can understand this quality. At times you may neglect family responsibilities and you may also feel guilty. You may instinctively know how to care for your child in a way that caters for everyone's needs within your family group, and your child may feel this too.

7 As a parent you may be teaching your child to connect with their inner sense of knowing, their wisdom, or "truth." They may have a perception about life very different from your own, but it is their truth. You may also be dreamy and imaginative at times and your child may help to keep you deeply rooted in physical reality. Spirituality may be one level through which you relate to your child.

8 As a parent you may feel a strong karmic bond with one or all of your children. At times you may like to inspire your children by being a strong parent. You may try hard because you may not want your child to be disempowered by any failure on your part, particularly materially, but you may also be teaching your child about inner spiritual values, and that "failure" in life doesn't exist if you are learning lessons from your experience.

9 As a parent you may be teaching your child to be liberal and to treat all people the same. Perhaps you are an authoritarian parent, who often tells your child what is right or wrong. You may also share your joy of knowledge and learning with your children, though you may have very high expectations of your children, which they may rebel against at times.

BELOW As a parent with an 8, you may like to inspire your children with your strength gained through experience.

ABOVE Lover
Number 6, you are
a pure romantic
at heart.

LOVERS

1 With a 1 in your chart you may be an ambitious lover, who draws your partner close to you intimately and perhaps likes to lead the way. You may enjoy conquering your lover or surrendering to the passions between you, but you may also be single-minded in achieving satisfaction in a self-centred way. As an ideas person, you may also devise many ways to make your love life interesting.

2 With a 2 you may like to negotiate what, where, and how you are going to make love so that you feel happy knowing that you both consent. This is because harmony is important to you and also because you are a caring and considerate person who likes to please others. You are a thoughtful lover, although you can also be demanding when it suits, and complacent at times too.

3 With a 3 in your chart you may be an uninhibited lover, and if your lover has never blushed then you may give him or her a good opportunity to do so. Your sense of humour may help to put your lover at ease, along with light-hearted banter that distracts him or her from any feelings of insecurity. You

may ooze confidence, which means that your lover may feel good around you.

4 You may be very passionate, especially when you feel secure with your lover and within yourself. This may be one reason why you turn to good friends, whom you already know for love. You may have endurance and therefore you may want to satisfy yourself and your lover many times over. Sometimes your love life may seem like a struggle, but you may put in much effort to make it work.

5 As a lover you may want your love life to be full of constant thrills, adventure and excitement, so your lover may need to be able to keep you on your toes. Indeed you may relish spontaneity and feel restricted if your lover can't provide the variety you need. You are able to give as much as you get, although it may be you who wants more and more!

6 As a lover you may like hearts and flowers, wonderful music, subtle lighting and all the things that create a perfect atmosphere where you can nurture your love life. You may like all the trimmings, and not feel fully satisfied or loved if they are left out. You enjoy all the tinsel and glamour but know that the carnal desires you exchange with your lover are important too.

7 With a 7, as a lover, you may enjoy sharing your love life with someone you feel emotionally and spiritually connected with and whom you can trust. Another part of you may also feel detached and therefore you may be only too happy to get involved with a lover who comes and goes, allowing you space. You may be dreamy and imaginative and use these qualities to enhance your love life.

8 As a lover you may like to be decidedly active or passive, and this may mean that you either do the seducing or love to be seduced. Your love life may seem like a power game at times, when both of you want to take control, and you can be really obstinate about what you want. Your lover may need to learn to appeal to your ego to make the most out of your love life together sometimes.

9 You may be an intelligent lover, who thinks through what your lover needs and then aspires to deliver and you may have wonderful bedside manners. You may be generally liberal in your attitude but prudish if you are asked to perform certain specialities; you may simply refuse. High expectations may also ruin a good love life, but you are adaptable and giving too.

FRIENDS

1 You may be a strong individual and all the people in your social circle may be similar. You may enjoy being the first to do something: the first to start your own business, or the first to wear the latest trend in clothes. It may also be that your group of friends has a pioneering spirit and you enjoy trouping around together, finding new things to do together.

2 With a 2, relating to your friends emotionally may be really important to you. Perhaps you can relate to some better than others, but you may generally see more of those with whom you have something in common, and with whom you can speak to easily. You may also have an extra-special friend whom you share many of your thoughts with, and you may choose to spend much of your time with him or her, because 2 highlights sharing and doing things two by two.

3 You may enjoy friendships with those who can make you laugh or share the same sense of joy and laughter. Perhaps you enjoy making friends on a superficial level where you can party and chat to them till late at night, yet they may never know that much about you. You may like friends with whom you can relax, particularly if you lead a busy and active life.

4 Loyalty is one of the key qualities you may offer or look for with your friends and you may go to great lengths to stick by them, though you may not always enjoy the dramas which may surround some of the friendships in your life. You may like to do practical things to help your friends, and you may also appreciate this quality in them.

5 You may like friends who speak "the same language", and your gift of communicating with a variety of different people may be strong. You may also enjoy friendships with people who like travelling, or who enjoy stimulating conversation. Flexibility may be a quality you admire in others, as it allows you freedom to be adaptable too.

BELOW With a 3, you thrive on being among friends with the same fun-loving outlook.

ABOVE Your broad range of friends is reflected in how openly you view the world; Number 6.

6 You may enjoy friendships with people with whom you can get dressed up in the trendiest clothes and head off into town to eat at the latest café, or see a movie, or visit an art gallery. Perhaps you find cultural events stimulating and enjoy getting fully involved in other people's ways of lives. Your range of friends may be broad, but they may all have a place of honour in your heart.

7 With a 7 you may like to have friends around with whom you can talk about the deeper and more philosophical issues in life, and you may seem wise about many of these things too. Friends may also respect your need to be quiet or alone for periods of time, but they also know when it is time for you to come out and party, such as when you isolate yourself from life too much.

8 You may like to surround yourself with friends who have some form of status that you admire, such as wealth or material possessions, because it may make you feel powerful, though another part of you may have no need for external riches; your friends may simply be rich in spirit. You live in the material and spiritual worlds, which may be reflected out in your choice of friends.

RIGHT Number 7; you are grateful to friends who help bring you out of yourself when you are being too introspective.

9 You may be very easy-going and get on with practically everyone, so you may also be relaxed about your choice of friends. You may feel that you can learn something from everyone you meet and the broader your outlook the better you may believe. Your friends may love to make arrangements for social activities with you, because you often fall in with their plans and adapt to the occasion.

COLLEAGUES

1 At work you may enjoy relationships with people with whom you feel can lead you further towards your goals. You may waste no time getting to know them. This can operate in a self-centred way, but if you work for a business this ambition may help to drive the whole company to success and therefore benefit everyone. You may also be a real comrade to your work associates.

2 With a 2 you may enjoy collaborating on projects with a colleague, making joint decisions and working closely with them. This is teaching you to relate to people, even in the instance that you do not relate emotionally. You may also be cautious of revealing your feelings to those at work and be touchy if you are asked to share your feelings.

2

3 You may not feel the need to get close to your work associates, but with your usually optimistic attitude and your happy-go-lucky nature you may rate high in the popularity stakes and you may enjoy expressing yourself or enjoy a good gossip with those at work. Sometimes you can be critical of people and how they perform.

4 You may be a dependable person, somebody whom people rely on in the work place. You may take your responsibilities seriously and work hard to follow them through, and you may put the same effort into work relationships too. Sometimes you can be hard to deal with because you may set your boundaries so tight.

5 You may work in an environment where people stimulate you with new information, and this may have a magnetic attraction for you. You may love to learn and are curious about life, and work is a good place to learn. You may realize that everyone has a story to tell and that you can widen your knowledge.

6 At work you may enjoy the comforts of knowing that you are part of a team environment, with a team spirit, while working towards collective goals. You may find that you get involved deeply with the social issues of people in your group.

7 You may be very observant and with your keen intuition know best when to keep quiet or to speak to people at work. Perhaps your work associates admire your sensitivity. At other times you may be a real catalyst who puts the cat among the pigeons by revealing your honest feelings. You may find important issues at work involve trust, because this is one of your major lessons in life.

8 You may have a well-developed intellect and enjoy relating to work associates on a mental level. Perhaps you relate to them by discussing work topics or your latest achievements or the company's ambitions. You may want to stay in control, so you may keep the conversation fixed firmly on subjects you understand or direct them in a way you want them to go.

9 You may inspire your work associates with your fairness and non-judgemental attitude – some of the time. Perhaps you are popular because you are so accepting of others' faults and simply accept them as they are. You can also be critical, and on the rare occasion that you lose your temper it may really shock! You may also be warm and caring with everyone.

COMPARING NUMBERS

★ ★ ★ ★ ★ ★ ★ ★ ★ ★ ★ ★ ★ ★ ★ ★ ★ ★

WHEN COMPARING YOUR chart with someone else's you first need to work out all your major numbers, and then do the same for them. To start with, you may be satisfied simply to compare Personality Numbers, or First Names, perhaps because you do not have the full information you need or because that level interests you most. It is helpful to read all about each number and what it relates to under the appropriate heading in this book before you do a comparison chart, understanding that Personality Numbers highlights psychological patterns of behavior, for example.

When comparing charts, let your intuition and inner wisdom play significant roles in reading between the lines. The information on these pages is simply a taste of the potential for each category. All the major numbers in your chart interact in a way unique to you, and it is the same for the person whose chart you are comparing. Here are listed basic clues to the lessons or qualities you may be teaching each other; there are many more.

One section compares odd and even numbers, a simple guideline to compatibility. Other categories highlight compatibility upon each of the physical, emotional, mental, and spiritual levels, to which you relate together. You are in the relationship to teach each other about different aspects of yourselves and broaden your knowledge of life. Challenges become strengths and strengths may continue to help you along your path in life.

One of the things that becomes apparent is that you do not need to try to match yourself to the same dominant numbers. Very different qualities can complement each other well. You may, for example, have a predominantly mental energy and your partner a physical one. The combination can make a very exciting relationship. Whatever the qualities of the two people, there will also be potential challenges in the relationship with which you can both identify.

1

RIGHT Compare your chart with someone close to you – it's fascinating!

ODDS

Odd numbers such as 1, 3, 5, 7, and 9 are active numbers associated with the quality of yang, which signifies the light side of life, the light within, and daytime. Everyone has degrees of yin and yang within them, the balancing act of nature that has made you who you are today. These numbers in your chart do not mean that you literally go around smiling and being angelic all day because you are basking in the light; you may need to learn to open up to the light as much as to the shadow side within you. Perhaps you find being in the light overpowering, like being on stage with all the spotlights turned on you at once, which feels hot and unbearable.

For example, with a number 9 in your chart, you may feel that you do not deserve the light or goodness at times, or you may feel that the light is everywhere, in everyone, and you may try to see something positive wherever you go and whoever you meet.

EVENS

In numerology the numbers 2, 4, 6, and 8 are passive or receptive energies associated with yin, the shadow within or night-time. This may mean that you are more likely to be aware of your shadow side and perhaps be more prepared to look within at the qualities and lessons that need to be brought into the light and transformed. For example, with an 8 you may re-evaluate life a great deal and be more open to challenging these shadow qualities. You may be so acutely aware of the shadow side that you make an effort to focus on the positive or the

lighter aspects of life. You may also sometimes get overwhelmed with negative or shadow aspects contained within your chart; for example, becoming bogged down with your emotions if you have the numbers 2 or 6 in your chart, or becoming burdened with responsibilities with the numbers 4 or 8.

LEFT Living in the spotlight is a means of relating to the active, yang qualities within you.

COMPARING ODD AND EVEN (MAJOR) NUMBERS

Odds and Evens

Opposites attract and if one of you has a good deal of yin energy and the other has a good deal of yang energy, this is especially the case because together you make a whole. Life is also asking you to find a sense of wholeness within yourself and, in order to learn about the polar opposite qualities, you have attracted this relationship to you. This relationship can work really well when you both have defined roles and stick to them, but life is constantly moving and changing, and so are you. Each of the seasons in the year helps to balance out your yin or yang energies. Because odd and even numbers are so different you may find that you rub up against each other more than other numbers in the equation, which allows for as much work to be done on personal development.

BELOW Yin and yang. Active and passive energies make up life.

ABOVE A combination of chords creates a harmony. This also relates to couples who take a positive attitude toward each other and life.

Evens with Evens

When you are in a relationship with someone who has the same number as you (in whichever area of life) you are conveying to the world that you are looking for a harmonious and peaceful life, qualities both contained within the numbers 2 and 6. You can still teach each other many lessons, but the relationship may seem less dramatic and much calmer than the odd and even combination. These numbers do have challenges of their own, of course. The Number 4 highlights drama, though you can be very down-to-earth and remain calm in a crisis. In order to achieve harmony together you may go through periods that are not always rosy, but you may both be receptive to life and learning, and these qualities can help to sustain your relationship. All even numbers reflect receptive energy and are yin in principle. This relationship may have a calming influence over you, and this may seem very much part of a healing process, particularly where relationships are concerned.

Odds with Odds

Two people with yang or active energy may be as compatible as two people with yin energies, though there may be more fire contained within this relationship. Perhaps you both have strong views about what you want or do together, but each of you can also empower the other with this quality. With an odd number in your chart you may like to think that this relationship is leading you somewhere, and this may particularly be the case with 1s in your charts. In life you tend to get further by looking inside yourself first, and you may be a catalyst in helping each other to look at the deeper aspects of life. This also includes examining your shadow side, which you are helping each other to transform, even though you may resist this at times. You may be compatible when you both think that you are heading in the same direction, but at other times it may seem like you are shooting off in entirely different directions.

COMPARING LEVELS OF COMPATIBILITY

Your major numbers can have physical, emotional, mental or spiritual qualities:

Physical	4, 5
Emotional	2, 3, 6
Mental	1, 8
Spiritual	7, 9

Physical with Physical

You may both enjoy learning to relate to each other physically, perhaps by hugging or touching, or by undertaking practical work together on issues or projects. One of your jobs is to help to keep each other's feet planted firmly on terra firma and to be realistic about life and this relationship. You may both be able to encourage and help each other deal with the practical and material aspects of life. In this relationship, loyalty is high on the agenda, for which you both need to make time and effort, and you may be aware of this. You may challenge each other's sense of security at times.

Physical with Emotional

When one of you is preoccupied with an emotional challenge in your life, the other may offer practical solutions to help you to center yourself and look at the situation in a down-to-earth way. This combination can work well, with the emotional energies of one person bringing warmth and feeling into the relationship and helping bring out the passion for life in the physical person too. Challenges in this relationship arise when one person is locked into their emotions too much and the other is locked into their insecurity of materially surviving in the world. Personal dramas that may occur can sometimes help to clear the air in this physical–emotional dynamic.

Physical with Mental

With a 1 or 8 in your chart, indicating mental energy, you may be dynamic and have a bright, active mind, and a strong will, and be very creative. The physical person can help to ground the ideas and energy of the mental person, a combination that may make this relationship very exciting indeed. With physical energies influencing this relationship, there may be some resistance to being together emotionally, but the collective will of you both helps to set your joint agenda. Perhaps you both think too much about things, so the physical energies may help to take you forward in a more practical, measured manner.

Physical with Spiritual

One of you is influenced by spiritual energies, so you may like to be free to roam around in your mind in order to connect with your inner self and your spirituality. Challenges may occur in this relationship when the physical person sets excessively rigid boundaries about times you need to meet or be together, but this structure can also help the spiritual person to function in the material world. Sometimes, with physical energies combining with spiritual energies, you may feel that there is too much emphasis on physical results rather than the spiritual growth of the relationship or vice versa.

ABOVE Mutual interests can help bring people together.

LEFT Complement your partner's emotional needs by offering helpful practical advice.

ABOVE You are learning to relate to each other emotionally.

Emotional with Emotional

You are strongly teaching each other to relate on the emotional level and feel safe to access deep feelings you can share together. Your relationship can be compatible when both of you understand how each other feels, but it can also be challenging when you are both feeling overemotional. You may find that you feel strongly attracted to each other as a friend, lover, or work colleague because of this deep emotional connection, and you may indeed wish to spend much of your time together. You may both be touchy at times and perhaps avoid each other when you have to discuss issues that are perhaps more sensitive.

Emotional with Mental

With emotional and mental energies combining in this relationship, you may both be able to access your feelings and discuss them openly with each other, while also being able to apply an active mind to help you rationalize your feelings. Sometimes the mental energies of one person may be such that they want to dominate the emotions of the other by playing feelings down, perhaps so that they do not need to connect with their own uncomfortable feelings. At other times, when one person is wallowing in their emotions, this can prove a challenge for the other person and they may not know what to do, though they may bring some logical thinking in to help resolve the situation.

Emotional with Spiritual

There may be a great deal of emotional sensitivity within this relationship, because the person with spiritual energies may feel deeply about life. This may also provide for a very caring relationship with great awareness given to the feelings of each other. Sometimes, when one person is being emotional, the other may have a strong connection to him or her spiritually and be able to share their wisdom or help give them guidance. If the spiritual person looses their sense of inner connection for a while, the other may be able to help them contact any feelings which may be blocking their overall situation.

RIGHT You help each other put your feelings into perspective.

Mental with Mental

You may both have strong minds and take it in turns to be a pillar of strength to each other within this relationship. There may be a meeting of minds on many issues, but where you don't connect you may set up power games or find means to get your own way, so flexibility may be required within this relationship, as well as a need to identify each other as individuals so that you can teach each other to respect your different needs. One or both of you may also need to learn to be more assertive in going for what you want within this relationship.

Mental with Spiritual

It is often said that the greatest strength is found in feelings of vulnerability, and you may find this quality within your lives and your relationship together. When you introduce the spiritual elements to a logical mind or to any mental energies, it can help you to understand the deeper meaning and significance of this relationship and life more clearly.

Challenges may arise in your relationship if one of you resists seeing through your individual power and authority to their greater significance.

Spiritual with Spiritual

Within this relationship you may both feel a deep spiritual connection to each other and also to life. You may go beyond your everyday connections with each other and observe the deeper lessons of humanity, too. Challenges may occur if you both refrain from paying sufficient attention to practical issues arising in this relationship. By always looking for a deeper meaning to situations, you may miss the obvious lessons that life is teaching you when you are together.

ABOVE LEFT You may both have strong minds and think the same.

ABOVE Vulnerability can soften a logical mind in a partner.

LEFT You may help each other get in contact with your spirituality.

PART THREE

HEALTH AND LIFESTYLE

★ ★ ★ ★ ★

In this fast-moving world, finding time to relax and to develop your own lifestyle is sometimes both a necessity and a chore. But learning to look after yourself and enjoy life is a gift which everyone can experience. Of course, feeling joy in life comes from within and is not dependent upon what external things happen to you or what you do each day. This relaxation from within can be experienced when we pursue pastimes that we enjoy.

The different elements that combine to make our lifestyles more purposeful include our culinary tastes, the type of vacations we take, sports and therapies that may help us to relax, and our state of health. The environment around us, from gardens and animals to the music we listen to, all contribute to developing a harmonious lifestyle in which we feel inpsired to live. Numerology provides the key to these elements, and helps identify the environments that best suit our individual needs.

BELOW Each person's numerological chart can help identify leisure pursuits that most appeal.

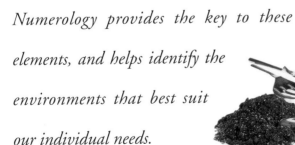

HEALTH AND MEDICINE

∗∗∗∗∗∗∗∗∗∗∗∗∗∗∗∗∗∗

Numbers influence everything, including your health, and it is interesting to note the names of medicines, both allopathic and complementary, to see the information they reveal about their properties, and the conditions they are meant to help.

Perhaps in the future traditional doctors and therapists will be able to study in detail the methods of numerology, both in their diagnosis and recommendations, and also in the timing of when patients take specific medicines. Some systems around the world, including the ayurvedic system, advise that their natural medicines be taken at certain times of the moon cycles. Many complementary therapies that use color essences or flower essences have numbers for the names of these natural medicines. This is useful additional information, which when aligned with the professional knowledge of any allopathic or natural medicine can be very helpful indeed.

Medicines pass in and out of popularity and have done so since time began. Numerology helps guide you to the trends of certain illnesses, such as the occurrence of epidemics and also highlights times when certain medicines may be more popular or may be used to greater potential as a result of alignment with the appropriate Universal Year number vibrations, or even the Monthly, Weekly, or Daily vibrations.

In this section of the book you can read about health trends, and what types of natural medicines you may be attracted to. Your choices are influenced by your Personality, Life Path, Soul, and Karma Numbers.

PHYSICAL LEVEL, NUMBERS 4 AND 5

Physical numbers in your chart mean that you may be down-to-earth, practical, sensible, and logical, with a keen grasp on reality. You may be hard-working, with great perseverance, able fully to take responsibility for yourself. You may also like communicating and being able to express yourself easily in the world. Sometimes you may also feel insecure and burdened by responsibility. You may also feel restless and be unpredictable and changeable, and you may pick things up and then drop them easily without thinking through the consequences. You may also feel resistant to changes in your life and at times feel like running away or being really irresponsible. You may visit a medical herbalist as earthy medicines from the ground, such as herbs, may attract you.

EMOTIONAL LEVEL, NUMBERS 2, 3, AND 6

You may be highly sensitive and use this in a positive way to help others. You may be very generous, warm, loving, and giving. You may search for peace and harmony in your life, though sometimes you give in order to keep the peace with

ABOVE St. John's Wort, often known as the Miracle herb, has a 2,400-year history of recorded use.

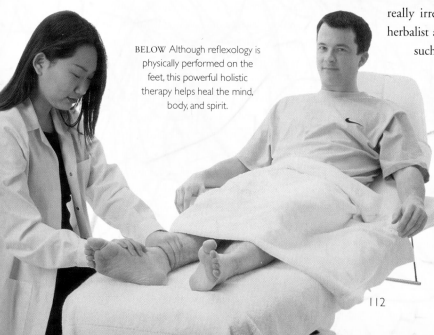

BELOW Although reflexology is physically performed on the feet, this powerful holistic therapy helps heal the mind, body, and spirit.

those around you. Tender and kind, you also like things to be fair so that there is a balance in life and your relationships that you are in. Your feelings are important to you and you may spend some time relating and sharing yourself with others. At times you can be moody and sometimes life may seem like an emotional seesaw. You can be too self-absorbed at times and get so selfishly carried away with how you feel that you fail to notice how others are feeling. Paradoxically, you may be inclined to give too much to others at times, even when you need time to yourself. You may like to visit an aromatherapist, as you may enjoy the sensual smell of the oils and also be attracted to their potential healing energies.

MENTAL LEVEL,
NUMBERS 1 AND 8

You may be bright, enthusiastic, energetic, and focused on what you want to achieve in life. You may be a dynamic leader, who is strong and independent, and you may be somebody who likes to be in control, of both yourself and a group. You may have lots of creative ideas, and a logical mind that helps you to solve problems. You may also be one of life's intellectuals, only too happy to engage in debates or stimulating conversation to exercise your mind. Charming, witty, and inspiring, you may really enjoy the spotlight and like being the centre of attention. At times you may be dominant and bossy and enjoy playing at being the boss in whatever company you keep. You may feel insecure, or feel the need to let others know when you are around. You may also like to leave your mark on any situation. You probably take your health problems first to your family doctor, but you may also visit a Flower Essence therapist, who understands the vibrational aspects of flowers for healing.

SPIRITUAL LEVEL,
NUMBERS 7 AND 9

You may be opinionated, sharp, shrewd, and able to hold your own. You may be quick-thinking, able to calculate what is needed for your next move. You may also be introspective and motivated to find the truth in life, and project an air of wisdom and knowledge. You may enter deep into discussion about philosophical issues. Religion and spirituality may interest you or be incorporated into your life, perhaps as you set aside time to ponder or attend a meditation class. At times you may be patronizing in your opinions of others, or feel superior to them; you can also be pretentious. You may also be dreamy and imaginative and become out of touch with the facts about life. You may feel the need to protect yourself in life as you can feel too vulnerable and open to the world at times. You may like to visit a homeopath, who understands how the mind, body, and spirit relate.

ABOVE In aromatherapy the scent and the beneficial psychological effect of essential oils go hand in hand.

BELOW The need to be touched is an essential and primitive human instinct.

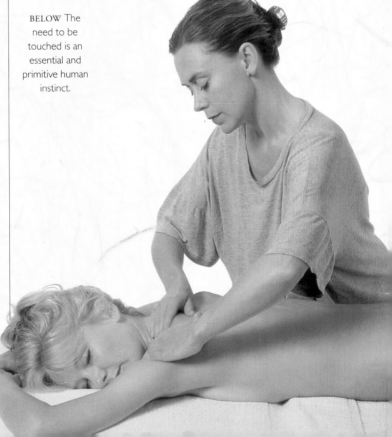

FOOD AND EATING

★ ★ ★ ★ ★ ★ ★ ★ ★ ★ ★ ★ ★ ★ ★ ★

EVERYBODY DIGESTS FOOD differently according to their constitution, their external environment, and their own internal process, which is ever-changing. Digesting food isn't simply about your physical body processing the foods, but about nourishment for your mind, body, and spirit.

In your personal numerology chart, particularly with the major numbers like your Personality and Life Path Numbers, you can see the kinds of foods you may enjoy eating. Enjoyment is the key to nourishing yourself with food as it works on all levels of your body. At specific times of the year, for example with the change in seasons, you may find that foods you are not normally attracted to suddenly end up on your plate. Love is one of the most important ingredients in preparing foods. When you eat something cooked by a lover in an angry mood you may have noticed it somehow doesn't taste nice, even when it is one of your favorite foods. Energy is food, and food is energy.

ABOVE Your constitution, state of mind, and surroundings may have an effect on the kind of foods you eat.

You may also notice that your taste buds change with each of the Personal Years you go through; for example, in a 3 or 6 year you may be attracted to rich dairy foods. You may also find that you go through life eating certain foods, then dropping them for a while, then picking them up again. If you study your numerology cycles carefully you may well find these go in 9-year cycles. You may also identify food with circumstances. If you are experiencing a 6 Personal Year and eat a lot of candy, then everytime you go through a 6 cycle, be it a 6 Day, Week, Month, or Year Cycle, you may eat copious amounts of it again. This is because you may be looking for some sweetness in your life, though you can absorb this in other ways apart from eating foods. Numerology can therefore help you to observe your eating habits, and what foods attract you, and see the psychological patterns of behavior associated with foods from the numbers in your chart.

FOOD AND YOU

Work out all the major numbers in your chart, followed by your Personal Year Number, then look them up below to see what kinds of foods you may sometimes want. Remember, you may have a combination of numbers in your chart, which may be expressed in your choice of foods at different times of the day or from year to year. You may also at times eat foods opposite to the types you regularly eat or to those that are listed.

1 With a 1 in your chart or as a Personal Year vibration, you are influenced by the element of air, which may mean that you enjoy light and airy foods. Perhaps you like rice cakes, whipped mousses, or seafood. The Italian diet of fish and vegetables may suit you well.

You may enjoy creating an extravagant feast for special occasions and be really inventive with your recipes, but most of the time you may like your foods to be easily prepared. You may be more likely to buy a takeout (or get it delivered), or prepare food which is already half-way ready, such as microwave food, rather than go to the trouble of cooking for yourself.

You may not be too bothered about esthetics as long as you get what you want. Food is food to you, whether it comes in pretty wrapping or not. Sometimes you may compulsively carry on eating long after your stomach is full, and you probably enjoy devouring every mouthful. When you eat out you generally prefer exclusive restaurants.

2 With a 2 Personal Year or major number, you have the element of water influencing you. Therefore you may find that you drink or eat foods with a high water content: perhaps ice lollies or fruit in summer, simple salads, or fruit and vegetable juices throughout the year. You may particularly enjoy bean sprouts.

You may invest much thought in what you eat and how you prepare foods for others. Indeed, you may have already read a lot of cookbooks about healthy eating and suitable foods, and established their nutritional contents. You may generally prefer simple foods.

You may like to eat in an harmonious environment, perhaps in a quiet place, particularly with one other person to whom you feel emotionally close. Sometimes you eat according to your emotions, so your food consumption may vary accordingly. Bars and restaurants may both appeal, and you may like the décor to be simple, just like your favorite foods.

3 With a 3 as a major number, or Personal Year Number, you have the element of fire influencing you. Perhaps you enjoy hot foods such as curries, spices, tangy foods, or Indian or Caribbean foods. You may also have a penchant for meat or rich foods, and boxes of chocolates may be the sort of impulse buys you would indulge in.

You may be a highly creative person, able to throw a meal together easily. Perhaps you enjoy preparing a variety of different foods even for one meal, so you may spend a good deal of time in the kitchen. You may be one of the lucky people who find cooking even the most complicated dishes easy.

You may enjoy going to bars and eating out at casual places that you just happen to stumble upon in your neighborhood or while you are on the road.

4 With a 4 as a Personal Year or major number in your chart, you have the element of earth influencing you. Earthy foods you may enjoy include root vegetables, pulses like lentils and beans, nuts, and grains like wheat and rye. You may also enjoy using fresh herbs, particularly if they are picked from your own window box or garden.

You may have a very practical approach to food, and before you cook a meal work out how long it will take you to buy the ingredients, then prepare and cook the foods, so that all is ready for your meal or your guests. You may be methodical and enjoy following recipes meticulously. You may generally like to make meal-times into a routine which can help you execute other daily tasks more smoothly. You

LEFT Cravings for certain foods may be traced through personal numerological cycles.

ABOVE Those with a 2 as a Personal Year may enjoy foods which contain a high water content, such as healthy garden vegetables.

may go out of your way to make the meal itself special by decorating the table artistically and creatively. You may also enjoy making lunch-boxes and taking home-made foods to eat out-doors as a picnic.

5 With a 5 in your chart or as a Personal Year Number, you have the element of air influencing you. You may enjoy foods which are light, or eat little amounts of foods, but more often. Air foods include souflées, some Chinese foods such as noodles and salads, rice cakes, and light and airy sponge cakes. You may also experience food addictions at times.

You may love to cook, because you enjoy bringing all the wonder-ful ingredients together and seeing the results, particularly when your guests congratulate you on your successful efforts. You can also run out of steam as you try to be too adventurous in your preparation of a meal, though surprising your guests may be one of your talents.

You may be a sensual person so the lighting, music, temperature, and smell of the room, and the way you are dressed may all contribute toward dictating whether you enjoy a meal or not. You may be prone to running around with food in your mouth, as you don't make time to sit down and eat. You may be as likely to eat out in an expensive restaurant as in a back-street diner.

6 With a 6 as your Personal Year Number or major number, you have the element of water influencing you, so foods with a high water content may appeal. You may enjoy a macrobiotic diet, with its high vegetable and mineral content, as well as foods from the sea, such as certain seaweeds. Healthy wholefoods may also appeal to you.

You may be a perfectionist, so you may take a long time laboring over the preparation of foods and do it in a caring way. You may love to nurture yourself and others; this pleasurable energy transmits into your food and the recipes you make. You gen-erally enjoy cooking as much as eating the foods you create.

Along with the beauti-ful foods you prepare, you may also enjoy creating a sensual envi-ronment at meal-times. Perhaps you have pictures of food and flowers hanging on your walls, which all add to the color and wake up your senses. You may like dining where you know the staff will really look after you.

7 With a 7 as your Personal Year or major number, you have the quality of water influencing you. You may enjoy foods with a high water content, such as fruit and vegetables and also regularly cook foods that require lots of water, such as porridge or rice. Japanese food, like sushi, may also appeal, and you may be fussy about what you eat.

You may be meticulous in your preparation of foods: clean hands and apron, scrubbed work surfaces, polished cutlery, pristine dinner service, and serving utensils may be important. You may also like to time things so that the food arrives at the dinner table for your guests at the best possible time. Your approach may even be clinical at times.

You may be a loner, so you may actually enjoy eating in your own company. Your brilliant organizational skills can at times be put to great use entertaining dozens of guests at once, which you may also enjoy. When you dine out it may be in well-chosen restaurants by personal recommendation only.

8 With an 8 as your major number or Personal Year Number, you have the element of earth influencing you. You may enjoy earthy foods such as nuts and pulses; Indian dahl, breads, or potatoes. However, the traditional British meat and two veg may also appeal to you.

It is likely that you may have taken a cookery course on how to cook really complicated, delicious dishes because you may like to impress others, or you may have studied cookbooks in great detail. This means that you may be set on preparing foods in an elaborate way or be able to turn even the most simple foods into visions of ecstacy. Food power may be the way you play your game.

You may be set on inviting people to your home who are smart enough to realize what an amazing cook you are! You also like to show you're the best. Your table may also be generously laden with the best or the most expensive co-ordinated decoration you can find. Why go out to dine when the Michelin Star chef could be yourself?

9 With a 9 as your major number or Personal Year Number, you have the element of fire influencing you. You may particularly enjoy meats of all kinds, hot or cold, including German delicacies hot spicy foods such as Indian curries may also appeal to you. You probably enjoy eating really tasty foods.

When it comes to foods you may have high standards, and when you are preparing them, you may wish to make sure that you have all the right utensils to hand. You may also particularly enjoy cooking traditional foods from your local neighborhood. Paradoxically you may sometimes be so laid-back that you enjoy eating food right out of its packets or containers.

You may at times only enjoy your food when you know your cooking has satisfied others; this is true whether your guests have raved about your splendid dinner or even if they say they like it just because they are being polite – both these responses go some way to pacifying you. You may go a long way to ensure that the food you serve is well matched for your guests, and may often cook far too much. On a day off, bar food may appeal.

ABOVE Those with a Personal Year 5 could be eager to impress guests with sweet delights.

ABOVE Combining the element of earth with a 4 Personal Year Number may induce you to eat outdoors with family or friends.

PREGNANCY AND BIRTH

* * * * * * * * * * * * * * * * * *

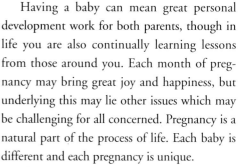

PREGNANCY IS A time for major change and transformation. And this is not just for the woman – a partnership undergoes a lot of changes. For a woman the physical body changes dramatically, and for both parents the emotional, mental, and spiritual levels are affected. In numerology, 9 months of pregnancy highlight the complete 1 to 9 cycle and in this section you can see general trends associated with each number.

Babies are sometimes born before or after the 9th month, perhaps because they are aligning with their family's collective energies or the universal energies of what is going on in the world. At other times they may be aligning with their parents' numbers. For example, if the mother's Life path Number is an 8, then he or she may be born in the 8th month, on the 8th, or with another compound number that adds up to an 8. Of course, a child generally has numbers they have received from both parents contained in their chart (particularly from their major numbers), so you may not be aware of the significance until the date the baby is born.

In some Eastern philosophies a baby is said to be born after 10 full lunar cycles. This is significant in numerology as the number 10 highlights the quality and the concept of rebirth. When you arrive at the number 10, you are yet again influenced by the number 1, because 10 adds up to a 1, highlighting new beginnings, fresh starts, and new goals. In life everything always ends back at a number 1, which in turns stems out of the potential contained within the 0. It is easy to see why 10 lunar months, may be regarded as the way of measuring the full term of pregnancy.

ABOVE From conception to birth, pregnancy is a time for reflection and personal development.

RIGHT Numbers from both parents are contained in the baby's chart; these are revealed when the baby is born.

Having a baby can mean great personal development work for both parents, though in life you are also continually learning lessons from those around you. Each month of pregnancy may bring great joy and happiness, but underlying this may lie other issues which may be challenging for all concerned. Pregnancy is a natural part of the process of life. Each baby is different and each pregnancy is unique.

If you are pregnant, look up your Personality, Life Path, Soul, Childhood, and Karma Number, along with your Personal Year Number. When these numbers arise in the month (and also the week) of the pregnancy, then those specific lessons are intensified. For example, if your Soul Number is a 3 and you are in the 3rd month, then issues around this number energy may be stronger.

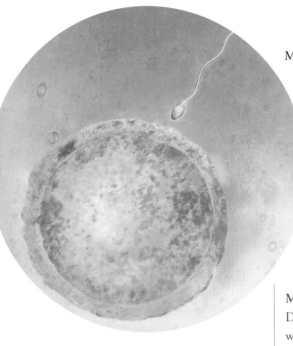

Month 1

You are on a new journey, which may seem long and distant at this stage of your pregnancy. You may have just found out you are pregnant at the end of this month. The number 1 influences new beginnings for you, your partner, and your baby too. The 1 is associated with the mind and the will; it also influences identity, which may be an issue during this month, where you may be also setting your goals for the months ahead.

Month 2

During this second month you are working toward finding harmony within yourself, but as a result of active hormones associated with the 2, life may feel topsy-turvy at times. This 2 energy is helping you to readjust and to find balance in your life with your new identity, feeling where this child can fit into your life. It also influences care and nurturing, important throughout the whole of your pregnancy. Many people do not share their pregnancy with others at this stage. This may be because of the influence of the 2 which highlights caution, decision-making, and a need to weigh up the situation. This 2 month highlights a need for extra care and nurturing and to allow yourself to share your feelings with those close to you, which may help you stay calm.

LEFT From the time you know you are pregnant, you can chart your numbers and interpret the issues they highlight each month.

BELOW In month 1, when you may only just be aware of your pregnancy, you and your partner may reprioritize your lives in preparation for a new life.

Conception '0'

Conception is the gift of life. From the first moments of your baby's life you are in a relationship with him/her. Space and time and the past lives of the parents, along with the child's, can help to determine the journey you will have together. As in life, not all concepts and ideas work or are successful, as chance and probability also play a hand. Conception is the gift of life, and from this time, or whenever you find out you are pregnant, you are in a relationship with the child, and the child is also in a relationship with you and those around you. It is unlikely that you will yet consciously know you are pregnant, but some women have a gut instinct that something is different, something has changed; they are sensitive to the way nature is preparing them for the changes ahead. Perhaps you may notice slight physical changes in your body, or you may act in ways which seem out of sync with your general characteristics. At this early stage these changes may go unnoticed, particularly if you are very busy or wrapped up in other aspects of your life.

RIGHT Month 3 highlights the need to relax and adapt gradually to the changes in your body and your emotional state.

BELOW Spontaneous food cravings in month 5 go hand in hand with the shifting energy of this number, from which you may also gain self-confidence.

Month 3

During the third month you may start to be aware of the physical changes in your body, high-lighted by the number 3, which influences expansion. This number influences joy, happiness, and a need to relax into your pregnancy and to allow it to flow in its own way. The 3 influences the need to learn to be adaptable to changes which occur, as all life is change, and life moves you forward. During this month you may adapt to a new diet or a different shape, and you may notice changes within your relationship with your partner. You may find that you laugh a lot, or let go of things which would normally annoy you.

Month 4

During this month you are consolidating your pregnancy and you may find that you begin to notice the weight of the baby more. Your body may begin to feel more cumbersome and diffi-cult to move around. You may also feel even heavier because of issues of responsibility and feel burdened at times by the thought of these. With the influence of the 4 you may start to sink down into your pregnancy, to feel com-fortable with it, and you may notice that you start to feel more passionate about life, too. You may find that during this month you begin to alter your day-to-day life and restructure it to suit your new needs. Perhaps you also feel like life is hard work, though the 4 influences staying power and the determination to carry on with all these new challenges.

Month 5

In the fifth month you may feel dynamic, and more attractive. Perhaps you feel like making love with your partner more often during this time. You may also develop cravings for certain foods; with the 5 influencing spontane-ity you may find yourself eating chocolate with your main meal! The 5 energy can be unpre-dictable and in this month you may find your-self doing or saying things without thinking. Perhaps you find that you become more adven-turous, like buying an unusual new dress. You may notice the restrictions of your physical body at this time and certain movements may seem really challenging. This 5 energy may shake up your life. You may never have felt more alive.

Month 6

In this sixth month you may feel more roman-tic; you may feel as if you need oodles of love and affection from your partner, or you may want more candlelight and roses. You may want to be spoiled and cosseted during this cycle. You may may also find you get into the glamour of being pregnant. You may like to buy clothes for the baby, decorate the nursery, and pay extra attention to your physical appearance. Perhaps at this stage you may also let go of looking perfect, and choose comfort-able clothes to wear. Your inner beauty radiates for all to see. With a 6 you may feel ultra-sensi-tive and become more emotional or sentimen-tal about life. Perhaps you wallow in your feelings or feel guilty about being so emotional. During this cycle you may have a strong desire to provide for your child and protect it.

Month 7

You have now experienced the first full 6 cycle of events and in this cycle you draw together your experiences into completion. In terms of your health, for example, if you have felt a little unsettled so far, then things may start to calm down now. You may feel as if the birth of your child is becoming more real; it is fast approaching and you may even start to panic about this on one level. This is the first physical stage of the baby materializing into form; medically it is said that at 7 months a baby generally has all its functions readily formed. The 7 highlights a deep spiritual connection now taking place particularly between you and the child, your partner, and the collective family. You may feel more in contact with your intuition and you may feel your baby's "being" very strongly indeed. You may also be more introspective, contemplative, and more vulnerable and emotional at this time.

Month 8

In the eighth month you may feel your inner or spiritual strength influencing you and giving you the will to carry on. You may feel challenged as this month highlights re-evaluation; at this stage you may be thinking more about who you were, who you are and who you may become. As these deep inner changes are taking place you may not identify with yourself at times. The number 8 influences a releasing of the past and a willingness to live in the present moment – to live your life for today. The 8 is a karmic number, so memories from past situations or of past lives may also flood over you at times. You may physically feel so heavy that you may wish your baby was born on the spot. Personal responsibility is also highlighted, along with a need to keep your mind focused, occupied, and positive.

ABOVE In month 9, motherhood is imminent and new beginnings make new demands on you.

Month 9

The number 9 influences endings and new beginnings, a transformation is taking place. You may also feel a strong spiritual connection and a deep bond to your child. Perhaps you also feel liberated that the end of your pregnancy is near or is now complete. Sometimes when things end you may also feel a sadness, a natural part of the process of moving forward in life. Your child will also be liberated from you physically, which can bring feelings of joy or loss. You may feel very emotional, or develop a fiery temper at times. Perhaps you become more argumentative as the 9's influence makes you agitated and ready to move on. You may sometimes feel great frustration as you wait in no-man's-land or in limbo, waiting for one thing to end and the other to begin. Humor may be essential during this final month of pregnancy, but luckily this is a quality of the 9, and so you should be able to keep smiling!

LEFT 8 is a karmic number bringing memories from the past, but teaches you to live in the present.

CHOOSING CHILDREN'S NAMES

* * * * * * * * * * * * * * * * * * *

BOYS NAMES

Christopher
Peter
Scott

GIRLS NAMES

Lucy
Sarah
Anna
Marie
Beatrice
Lorraine
Fiona
Eleanor
Caroline
Melanie

CHOOSING CHILDREN'S NAMES is a natural process, but it may seem challenging, particularly when you and your partner want to call your child by different names, or grandparents insist that you bring their names into the equation too. This can be a tricky business, perhaps with one partner giving in to the other's choice, or both compromising by fitting in middle names in the hope that this will make everyone happy. Right from the beginning of the pregnancy, you are able to instinctively tune into your child. As parents you are able to identify some of the characteristics your child may have.

There is a very logical approach to naming children that derives from the simple fact that a child takes genes from the mother and the father, so some numbers from both parents' charts will also be present in the child's numerology chart. For example, if one partner has a 17/8 Life Path Number and the other a 6 Personality, then perhaps the child might be born on the 17th or the 6th, or these numbers may show up in other areas of their chart, such as in their names. There may also be derivations of the child's numbers in the chart. Instead of a 17/8 the child may have an 8, or a 26/8, so that the single digit remains the same but the sub-influences are quite different.

Timing is also of great significance in highlighting the kind of numbers that may feature in a child's

chart. These can reflect issues that parents are working through around the time of conception. For example, if both parents were working strongly on relating together emotionally (associated with the number 2), you may find that the child has a lot of 2s in his or her chart, or that the number 2 and its derivations show up in one of his or her major numbers, as either a Personality, Life Path, Soul, Childhood, or Karma Number.

A child may also take on the energy of a number that needs to be brought out within the parents as part of their personal development work. For instance, if both parents find it a challenge to be direct (number 1) in their communication, then the child may be born with this in their chart, even as a major number. Perhaps the child will be very forthright or perhaps even more covert as this behavior is mirrored back to both parents later on. The same process occurs if one or both parents have "missing numbers" from their chart; these may show up in the child's numerology chart.

As a child grows up, at each stage of life you can see which numbers are influencing them more at any specific time by their physical appearance. Also, you may look at your 4-year-old and see he looks more like the mother or father, and when you look at the chart of the parent he or she most resembles you will see those characteristics reflected there; for example, with a 6 Personality a child may look fleshy and round, or with an 1 a child may look slender or even skinny.

RIGHT The choice in names for your child may seem endless. Tuning into your child's date of birth may help you make the best decision.

BELOW Remember that the full date on which your child is born holds the key to his or her future.

APRIL
THURSDAY
15

CHOOSING NAMES WITH NUMEROLOGY

You may think that if you want your child to be loving you will give your child a name with a 6 as this quality is contained within its potential, or an 8 may introduce business flair. Synchronicity plays a large part in life, so children develop in their own way and nobody can be completely sure how they will utilize the energies or numbers available to them. Even when children grow into teenagers or adults, they may be influenced by the numbers in quite a different way than when they were very young. Life is full of surprises and in numerology it is always the hidden potential contained within the numbers that has the strongest influence over your life.

If you do intend to choose a child's names by working them out with numerology, it is essential to first trust your instincts about what characteristics you feel the child has. A major clue about numbers you may choose arises from the major numbers in both partners' charts. Another clue arises from your child's date of birth, and it may be helpful to wait until the child is born to name him or her. Of course, if you have a child by Cesarean section, then you may even have the responsibility of choosing your child's date of birth too.

Sometimes during pregnancy, parents will choose a name, but when the baby arrives they find that it does not "fit" and they change it. At other times one or either of the parents will

LEFT First names and middle names are equally difficult to decide upon, but each will add up to a number which influences your child's potential.

choose a first name early on and then stick to it because it feels right. When you translate each letter into numbers and add them up you will see the qualities, strengths, and challenges they contain, and why you have chosen the numbers. It has been known for parents to change the spelling of a chosen name at the last minute. Again this is synchronicity at work, giving the child the best possible numbers he or she needs in order to learn their lessons in life.

POPULAR NAMES

When choosing the numbers for your child's chart, you may also be influenced by the Universal Year Numbers, the specific Year influencing you at the time. For example, in the year 2000, which adds up to a 2, you may find that lots of babies are given names that encompass this 2 energy. John or Sarah add up to 20/2. This explains the phenomenon of popular names, because people pick up the Universal Year energies reflected out through the children's names that are given throughout the world.

Life is a mirroring process, and naming children is part of this. It reflects the numbers in their parents' charts and the collective energies or numbers that are influencing everyone when they are born.

LEFT Children can teach you as much about yourself as you teach them.

CHILD'S PLAY

* * * * * * * * * * * * * * * * * * *

PLAYING IS FUN, particularly for a child. It is an important form of education, helping children to learn faster than many other methods. Play can also be very therapeutic, allowing children to channel their energies in a positive way and release stress. It can also stimulate your mind, body, and spirit, and can open up your awareness to life, no matter what your age.

You may like to work out your child's Personality Number and then look up this number in the section below. It can indicate activities to keep your child happily entertained, as well as other ways in which they may like to have fun and learn about life for themselves.

1 With a 1, children may like to play by reading a good book, perhaps about Robinson Crusoe or great explorers or subjects that make them think. The game of charades may appeal, where they act out a role from a book, a movie, or a play. This encourages them to think about different identities, and also helps them to utilize their creativity and fill their minds with ideas. They may easily be able to make up their own games and invent new ways of looking at old activities, injecting new life into them.

RIGHT Children with a Personality 2 may like to splash around in the bath.

ABOVE A Personality Number 3 indicates an imaginative child who finds great expression through painting or crafts.

RIGHT With a 1, children are happy to become absorbed in stories.

2 With a 2, children may like to play noughts and crosses, Scrabble, or games for two people. This may be because they love to share their activities with others,

and they may also like to have a special friend with whom to play. They may love music and perhaps play a musical instrument. Any kind of ball games may appeal, particularly tennis or rounders. They may also like to play in the bath; they may love splashing water, or making bubbles from a bottle of soap suds.

3 With a 3, children may love to play Consequences, where a story is narrated or written down and each person in the group adds their own little bit as the story unfolds. They may like dressing up as clowns, and create a dictionary of jokes to entertain others. They may love to make things with their hands, such as aeroplanes, dolls, jewelry, and collages, and they may use lots of different colors too. These children may enjoy making sculptures or objects out of clay, or love to paint or draw.

4 With a 4, children may love to play outdoors in the garden or park; perhaps they love climbing trees, playing on a slide, or scrambling frame, or romping around on a swing. They may love gymnastics,

where they can use their physical strength to negotiate apparatus and specific movements. Perhaps they enjoy exploring the garden by collecting leaves, branches, soil, and flowers, and have a fascination with the earth. Indoors they may love to build things, perhaps with bricks or out of paper. They like being practical.

5 With a 5, children may enjoy playing musical chairs or pass the parcel, both of which incorporate music and contain a strong element of surprise. They may love to dance and run around, sometimes inexhaustibly all day. They may love to hopscotch (where they hop, skip, and jump over a chalk drawing on the floor) or to play on their bicycles. Perhaps they may like to read adventure stories, tales of a traveling circus, or books about different countries and cultures around the world. Puzzles may also fascinate them and they may also like general knowledge quizzes and jigsaws.

6 With a 6, children may enjoy dressing up and playing doctors and nurses or vets, where they can play roles caring for people and animals. They may love to play with make-up or experiment by dressing up in adults' clothes as they potter around the house. Glamorous clothes and bright jewelry may also appeal. Perhaps they like to read animal stories, and they may particularly enjoy ones about horses and ponies, which they may re-enact with friends outdoors. They may love to pacify themselves by playing with soft toys, like cuddly teddy bears or dolls that they can dress up in wonderful outfits and show off to the world.

7 With a 7, children may love to play hide-and-seek, where one person hides and the others need to find them, or blindfold games, where the eyes are covered and they are spun around and need to catch other children who are constantly moving. They may enjoy magic games where they can conjure up illusions, or like to play the game of "I Pretend" where they narrate a make-believe story with their friends. They may love to make wigwams or tents, where they can have space to think.

8 With an 8, children may enjoy playing games about power and authority, where one child is the boss and takes charge of the others. Or perhaps they prefer to be the one being told what to do and take a submissive role. They may love to play any kind of board game, perhaps about property and finance, and they love the thrill of competing with someone else, even if they don't win. Computer games may also be high on their agenda, as these are fun and entertaining and may help to stimulate their thirsty minds.

9 With a 9, children may love to read anything and everything. As they love to learn, playtime may seem as if it is never-ending. Perhaps they love to draw and paint; cartoons may be favorites and face-painting may also appeal to their creative nature. They may particularly enjoy making or wearing masks, which can easily be taken off at a moment's notice and adapted to suit the mood of the moment. Perhaps they love to write their own stories or plays, or have an extensive vocabulary for their age.

LEFT Acting out the grown up roles is a preoccupation for children with a 6 Personality Number, and adopting teddy bears as favourite toys.

BELOW Number 9 Personality; you may discover children begin to read and write at an earlier age than expected.

COLOR VIBRATION

* * * * * * * * * * * * * * * * * * *

COLORS ARE RAYS of energy, and all of life is made up of these rays. In your own numerology chart each of the numbers 1 to 9 have their own rays, and if you have a compound number in your chart, then you have sub-ray influences too. In the example of the number 31/4, the 1 and 3 are sub-rays of the number 4.

In numerology you can see which colors are influencing you, and in what different areas of your life. For example, if your Family Name is a 6, then the colors associated with this number influence your whole family. You may find then that everyone in your family loves to wear green, or perhaps you resist this color to some extent in order to strongly adopt your own individuality within your family group. Many colors will be influencing you, but the most significant ones will come from your Personality Number, Life Path Number, Soul Number, and Karma Number. People whom you attract may also enjoy wearing or appreciate similar colors to you. They speak the same language of colour.

Color is very important within your relationships. It's lovely to hear your lover comment on the beautiful color dress you're wearing or tie. You may

RIGHT *"Rainbow."* Color influences your thoughts and feelings.

BELOW If your Family Name is a 6 you may wish to show your individuality by wearing a contrasting color.

also use colors (sometimes subconsciously) to make statements for people to leave you alone; the color red can sometimes give off a warning message. The psychology of color is very important and by appreciating all the numbers in your chart, along with your Comparison Numbers, then you can make the most out of all your relationships.

You may also prefer some colors for sleeping in or relaxing, while wearing other colors for working in, and different ones to travel in. When you are ill you may not want to wear your usual shades of colors, or you may want different shades around you, even craving a certain color when you are sick. When you are sick you go "off color," and if you look at your Personal Year Number, Month Number, or Day Number, then you may see why you choose to have certain colors around you. Have you ever noticed that when you go on holiday you may wear styles or colors of clothes that you wouldn't regularly wear at home? This may often result from the temporary vibration that could be influencing you.

Personal Year, Month, or Week Numbers highlight potential colors, that may be influencing you. If you have that number in your chart already, particularly as a major number, then it may influence you greatly. Colors also bring back memories, and your application and wearing of colors may also result from the natural cycles in your chart. For example, if you were in love in a 6 Personal Year and you were often wearing the color pink, then in your next 6 Year, 9 years later, you may suddenly wish to wear pink again. One color may be dominant

in your life for a long period of time; for example, if your Life Path Number is an 8, then you may find yourself frequently wearing the color black for many years.

If you are in tune with yourself, you are more likely to wear colors that complement your energy at that moment in time, which is why people say it is good to feel comfortable in what you are wearing. What they mean is that you can feel yourself wearing a specific outfit or color.

From your numerology chart you will see that different elements are contained within each of the numbers. In relation to color, if you have physical numbers influencing you (4 and 5), then you may like quite harsh colors. With emotional numbers (2, 3, and 6) you may enjoy primary, watery colors, which seem soft and gentle. If you have mental numbers influencing you (1 and 8), then you may enjoy clear or crisp colors. With spiritual numbers (7 and 9) then sometimes bright or definite colors may appeal. These are just guidelines, you can choose colors that appeal more to you at the time. (From your overall chart the numbers may bring out certain other color preferences, at different times in your day or your life.)

COLLECTIVE TEMPORARY VIBRATIONS FOR THE YEAR 2000

There are also universal energies that may be influencing you each day from the collective or from the whole of humanity. If you tune into the number of the day in the month, or the whole date, then your inner wisdom may guide you to the colors that are influencing everyone

NUMBERS AND COLOR ASSOCIATIONS

1	YELLOW	7	NAVY
2	CREAM/WHITE	8	BLACK, RED
3	BLUE	9	WHITE, BLACK
4	BROWN		(CONTAINS ALL
5	YELLOW/ORANGE		THE COLORS IN
6	GREEN, PINK		THE SPECTRUM)

too. Here is a list of the 31 days in the month for the year 2000; as the 2 influences the whole of the next millennium, these colors may, to some extent, have an important influence on this whole period.

YOUR NUMEROLOGICAL COLORS

1	RUST	18/9	TRUE RED AND WHITE
2	BRILLIANT WHITE, PRIMROSE YELLOW	19/1	CLEAR GRAY
3	WATERY BLUE	20/2	ROSE
4	GREEN-BROWN	21/3	COBALT BLUE
5	CRIMSON RED	22/4	SLUDGE GREEN
6	APPLE GREEN	23/5	MAUVE, PALE YELLOW
7	JADE	24/6	MAGENTA
8	DEEPEST BLACK	25/7	INDIGO, RUSSET
9	DARK GRAY	26/8	PEACH PINK, BLOOD RED
10/1	DEEP YELLOW	27/9	DARK NAVY, BROWN
11/2	GRAY-WHITE	28/10/1	TANNED GOLD
12/3	DUSKY GREEN	29/11/2	RADIANT ORANGE
13/4	VIOLET	30/3	DEEP BLUE
14/5	SKY BLUE	31/4	GRAY, WHITE
15/6	SPARKLING SUGAR PINK		
16/7	WATERY BLUE		
17/8	VIVID PURPLE AND GREEN		

LEFT With a Life Path Number 8, you may discover what influenced you to wear predominantly black clothes for so many years.

FASHION, CLOTHES, AND PERFUME

* * * * * * * * * * * * * * * * * * *

NUMEROLOGY CAN HELP you to understand why you may be attracted to certain clothes, while clothes can also help you work out the numbers in somebody's chart when you first meet them. This can be very helpful at a job interview or on a first date, and although people's styles can change, these can give you a clue to the numbers they are working with at that time. You may see that the man who has just invited you out is wearing very smart but casual clothes; perhaps he has a number 2 or 8 in his chart. You may also wish to dress to impress your date or your prospective employer if you so choose to.

Numerology can also provide guidelines as to what clothes may suit you too, at different times in your life. If your Personality Number is influencing you greatly you may find that you are more inclined to wear clothes and perfumes associated with this number. If your Soul Number is influencing you, then clothes relating to that number may even feel more comfortable to wear. Indeed clothes can help to bring out aspects within yourself.

Work out the major numbers in your numerology chart, along with your Personal Year Number, and refer to the list in this section. You may also like to read about general trends which have been evident in the 20th century to see why styles were popular at different times.

BELOW Fashion through the ages – numerology can trace the styles and trends from elegant chic to minimalist glamor.

RIGHT In the 1930s, clothes became softer and more feminine.

COLLECTIVE INFLUENCES OF THE 20TH CENTURY

1900s: Clothes in this era were long and dark, but could also looked sophisticated (a quality of the 1); a slightly prudish look remained (influenced from the 9) from the Victorian era.

1940s: Times were hard during the world's strained political climate, so the emphasis was on practical and hard-wearing clothing, or survival wear, which are all qualities contained within the number 4.

1960s: This year adds to a 16/7 and sexuality and nature were highlighted here, in evidence in the rising hem of the mini skirt and also in the preoccupation with glamor and beauty.

1990s: The liberated '90s when every look was in fashion and there was no real fashion statement, was the result of the 9, which contains all the numbers 1 to 9 within it.

WHAT'S IN YOUR WARDROBE?

1 With a 1, you may enjoy wearing loud clothes that show off your body. You may love to pose and pout as you show others how wonderful you look. You may wear clothes that are unique, daring, and stylish, but sometimes you may, paradoxically, wear understated clothes too. Sophisticated perfumes may appeal to your bright and intellectual mind too.

2 With a 2, you may like to wear matching clothes and accessories and look neat. You may enjoy wearing simple clothes, which are easy to wear and with your ability to color co-ordinate, you may not be short of things to put on. Open-neck collars and clothes that look smart and chic may also appeal to you, and you may also like to wear delicate, feminine perfumes.

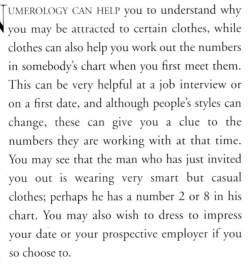

3 With a 3, you may enjoy wearing sportswear so that you can feel comfortable, relaxed, and free. This

does not mean that you go around in trainers all day, because you may be brilliantly creative and even make and wear your own designs. You may also be critical of your appearance and always want to look your best. You may wear perfumes which are light and uplifting.

4 With a 4, you may like to wear practical clothes to suit the occasion, whether dressing for a lover or for a business meeting, and you may generally like to look neat and orderly. At times you may break out of your routine and wear something extra special that may even shock others. You may like to wear perfume made from natural herbs or essential oils.

5 With a 5, you may like to experiment with your clothes and may even change them several times a day. Perhaps you wear trousers in the morning, a floaty outfit in the afternoon, and a sexy number in the evening. You may also put together leather and lace and enjoy the feel of both on your skin. You may be sensual and enjoy wearing musky perfumes.

6 With a 6 in your chart, you may like to wear clothes which look feminine in their appearance. Perhaps you like to wear flower print dresses in pretty colours, or more daring clothes that may accentuate your curves. Whatever you choose, you will always look feminine and well-dressed. Trendy clothes may also be well-stocked on your shopping list, along with the latest perfumes. Traditional rose may be a scent you admire, too.

7 With a 7, you may like to look crisp and sharp in your appearance, with everything in place; you may be very fussy about how you look. Perhaps you like wearing fussy clothes, or ones that seem to float off you. You have a vivid imagination and therefore you may design or wear the most incredible creations at times. Natural smells of perfumes, such as coconut or flowers may appeal to you.

8 With an 8, you may like to look intellectual, smart, and businesslike, or wear very sexy clothes, perhaps ones that cling to your body or have a revealing neckline. You may also like to wear smart pants or matching suits that make you look successful, rich, or powerful. Designer clothes may really appeal. Strong and sometimes overpowering perfumes may be your style.

9 With a 9, you may enjoy flamboyant clothing, with a loud liberal feel. You may also like to feel free to dress to suit your mood, or be rebellious in your choice of clothes at times, so as to stand out from the crowd. You may also like wearing clothes with a military feel to them, or polo necks and sweaters. Perfumes that bring out your animal instincts and passion may appeal – in particular heavy perfumes.

ABOVE Musky perfumes appeal if you are influenced by a number 8; they blend well with your sophisticated image.

LEFT With a 4 you are at ease with formal attire.

BELOW With a number 5 influencing your choice of garments, any occasion to dress up appeals.

VACATIONS AND LEISURE

* * * * * * * * * * * * * * * * * *

CHOOSING a form of vacation or destination can be quite a skill, particularly if you have to weigh up the desires and needs of other people. Numerology can help to guide you to the types of vacations, sports, and relaxation that may suit you, as well as the type of travel destinations that may be attractive.

Within your numerology chart you have five major numbers, but for this process you may wish to concentrate on your Personality and Life Path Numbers. You may also wish to add up your Personal Year Number, because this may influence methods you may enjoy and employ during that specific year. If people are traveling with you, then look at the same numbers in their Numerology chart too.

ABOVE An exhilarating adventure may induce a balance of adrenalin and relaxation in some people.

BELOW A simple beach holiday may fulfill your needs for relaxation.

1 You may be very physical and enjoy long-distance running, where you need to keep your mind and body focused, or you may take up jogging or aerobics. If you are goal-oriented you may enjoy competitive sports where leadership is also highlighted. Challenge is the optimum word with a 1 in your chart. You may like to go on holiday on your own, or, if you travel with others, do your own thing. You may go mountaineering, where your will and skills need to be matched, or you may pioneer and lead a rugged trip.

2 In order to relax you may simply slow down your regular routine and take a break by looking at a beautiful flower or picture. You may enjoy quiet or gentle exercise, such as simple stretches or swimming leisurely. You may even take up a low impact step class, or even do your work-out at home with a friend.

Travelling in twos so that you can share your experiences together may attract you. Outdoor destinations may appeal; you may enjoy yoga retreats where you can find your inner peace.

3 You may be an active person who takes up many different sports at once. Perhaps you enjoy jogging, cycling, or being a trailfinder, as you walk for relaxation in beauty spots around the world. You may also enjoy the social aspect of exercise, and do team sports.

You may enjoy the freedom to roam around on holiday and do all kinds of different things. A different destination every day of a holiday may well suit you.

4 Simple walking may be one of your favorite forms of exercise and relaxation, and you may may incorporate it firmly into your daily routine. Perhaps you also enjoy planning countryside walks. Weight-training may also appeal, as it shows tangible results that you can build upon in a step-by-step way.

You may enjoy vacations where you can keep your feet firmly on the ground. So a walking holiday in the mountains may appeal, or camping in the outback or countryside; horseriding may also suit.

5 With a 5, you may like to exercise with movement and enjoy dancing or an aerobics class set to music, so that you can step in time with the beat. You may enjoy being kept

on your toes. To still your active mind you may also enjoy meditation.

You may be a magnetic and fun-loving person who likes to holiday in groups – the more the merrier, you may say. You may also like to fit lots of short breaks into your year.

6 You may like to take up sports that make you feel good and allow you to dress up for the part. For example, you may be part of a water relay team, dressing up in sporty swimming costumes. You may particularly enjoy tennis, as it gives you a good work-out and you can look good, too.

You may take holidays at home, where you throw your doors open to your extended family and friends. You may also enjoy cultural trips, to cities like Vienna; a night out at the theater may seem like a holiday to you. Luxury hotels may also appeal.

7 Swimming may be one of your favorite exercises, particularly when your routine is undisturbed and you have the pool practicality to yourself. This is because with a 7 you need time to introspect, and to reflect in the stillness of your mind. T'ai chi or chi kung may suit you, but you may prefer their meditative aspects to the physical ones.

You may enjoy a holiday where you can find stillness or even solitude. Perhaps you like to visit spiritual centers or temples that can be found all over the world. You may also be impatient to see all the sights.

8 You may enjoy sports that require physical strength and stamina, so hurdling, sprinting, jogging, aerobics, and working out in the gym or with pilates may all appeal. One of your favorite sports may be riding, and you may turn this into a competitive activity at gymkhanas, cross-country meets, or with polo.

Sophisticated holidays may appeal, in a metropolitan city. Perhaps you spare no expense as you tour many of the best and most famous sights in town.

9 You may be very muscular, so that you are attracted to sports like swimming, javelin, football, badminton, squash, cross-country running, or anything that builds up your muscles and takes plenty of stamina to take part. If you are feeling mellow, then a laid-back game of tennis may suit your mood.

You may enjoy going on educational holidays with groups of people with similar interests. At other times you may like to head off into the sun, and sit under a canopy with a good book.

ABOVE With a Number 1, you may like to get away from it all.

TOP With a 3, you may need a physical activity to help you relax.

BELOW Group holidays appeal to those influenced by a 3, as this gives scope for social interaction.

POSITIVE STRESS

✶ ✶ ✶ ✶ ✶ ✶ ✶ ✶ ✶ ✶ ✶ ✶ ✶ ✶ ✶ ✶ ✶ ✶

STRESS IS A particular by-product of modern life, but people have always experienced stresses. Throughout history stress has affected people, and each generation has its own external ways of managing it. You may not even blink an eye or raise your pulse at circumstances that were stressful for your grandparents.

In one way, stress is the fear of new things, the resistance to move forward with your life even in simple ways, an avoidance of change. Stress may occur when you are not able to trust the process of life, which explains why you may get stressed even when seemingly positive events occur: the success of a company, marriage, the birth of a child. They all require you to go with the flow and can change your life in some way. The bigger the potential change, the more stressed you may become. Of course, stress can be a positive thing, driving you ahead in life and motivating you. Resistance is also a natural part of the process of moving forward because without something to push up against sometimes you may not be bothered to move on at all.

Sometimes resistance and stress may occur as a part of your natural make-up. In numerology, for example, this can be seen from friction between the influence of your Personality and Life Path Numbers, and particularly between your Soul and your Personality Numbers. When external stresses are evident in your life, you may like to look at the behavioral patterns and the lessons from all the major numbers in your chart to see what you can learn. Perhaps you are challenged by people who do not appear to be able to keep commitments in the office; your Life Path Number may be a 5, which highlights this issue, while your Personality Number may be a 4, and with its influences you may be loyal with your commit-

ments and complete them. There will clearly be a conflict in this situation which needs to resolved. When you work on your own personal development and change from within, it can dramatically influence your relationships and the kinds of experiences you may have in your life.

You are also as an individual under the influence of collective stress. Everyone is a part of humanity, one world, so you are always subconsciously connected and therefore under the influence of global stresses. Consciously you may be only generally aware of collective stress at home, in your local neighborhood, at work, or in places physically near you. These stresses can yet again be positive elements to drive you forward to help your community or to improve life with a positive attitude and actions.

Look up your Personality, Life Path, Soul, Childhood, Karma, and Personal Year Numbers to highlight potential trends associated with each number.

1 With a 1, you may be more aware of mental pressures in your life. You may get snappy, irritable, or even volatile. Exercise may help you to release mental stress; perhaps reading a fascinating book that grips your attention may help you to switch off from your preoccupation with your own problems.

ABOVE Number 9; if you forget things it may cause stress and frustration.

RIGHT Number 1; emersing yourself in a gripping novel can distract you from external pressure and help you relax.

2 With a 2, you may feel stressed from your emotions at times. Perhaps you sulk or daydream, or even cry, scream, and shout. When you are feeling emotional it may help you to reach out and help others around you. In doing so, you may forget your own feelings for a while.

3 With a 3 influence, you may be very sensitive – a person who worries about things. Perhaps you talk too much to push your feelings away or talk at people to keep them at arm's length. Sometimes being creative can help you to handle stress, like baking, painting, writing, or actively doing something.

4 A 4 stress may seem as if it is shaking your very foundations because you are a physical person who may like to feel your roots strongly anchored in the ground. Perhaps you try to cling onto situations more when you feel stressed or find that you eat more food to help you feel more secure. Having a meal out with friends and going for a walk may also help.

5 With a 5, you may feel the stresses from physical changes particularly. Perhaps you smoke or drink a lot, or take up habits that appear to cut you off from physical reality at these challenging times. A lovely massage or physical exercise may also help you relax.

6 With a 6, you may be instinctively sensitive to your environment and you are more likely to feel emotional stress, when you may let go of your appearance and take less personal care of yourself. Sometimes buying a new outfit or indulging in a beauty facial or manicure may help you to look good, and can really influence the way you feel about yourself.

LEFT Number 2, you may find solace in preparing a meal for family or friends.

7 With a 7, you may feel very stressed at times when it may seem that you have lost yourself or lost the spiritual connection with yourself and therefore to others. At these times you may by unapproachable, or oversensitive, or isolate yourself from the world. Talking to a close friend or even meditating with them may help you to feel connected again.

8 With an 8, you may experience mental anxieties as you try to work everything out in your head. Perhaps you frequently swear and curse at life or those around you. During stressful times it may help to do some gardening or get outdoors for some exercise. Perhaps you have your hair cut so that you can feel psychologically better snipping off your hair and bits of the past.

9 With a 9, you may feel collective stresses and pressures strongly and perhaps you feel a strong spiritual connection with those around you. Under stress you may become clumsy, forget things easily, or become resistant and angry. Going out for a drink with a group of friends may help.

BELOW With a Number 8, you may relate strongly to the rejuvenation of nature and find pottering in the garden very therapeutic.

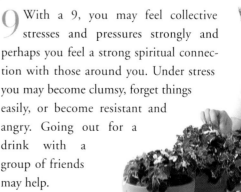

MEDITATION AND RELAXATION

* * * * * * * * * * * * * * * * * *

MEDITATION IS A form of relaxation and a way to reconnect with your inner self and your spirituality. It can also help you to feel more connected to others. There are many different forms of meditation, as well as a variety of experiences you may have while you are meditating. Each time you meditate it is different from the last because as a person you are constantly changing and you approach the day with a different perspective. Your situation at the time can also affect your reasons for meditating. Meditation is wonderful because it can help you to find inner peace and let go of some of the stresses of everyday life. It can also help to give you clarity or guidance about situations in your life, because when you meditate you may feel more closely connected to your inner self and your intuition.

Look at the major numbers in your numerology chart, as well as your Personal Year Number. See which types of meditation appeal to you or which may help you to relax.

BELOW Combining the soothing sound of dolphins with rhythmic breathing may provide a positive meditation programme if 2 is in your chart.

LEFT Your garden may provide peace and tranquility.

Meditation 1 With a 1 you may find you enjoy solitude and like to find a quiet spot away from the world to let you tap into your mind. Perhaps you may enjoy meditating first thing in the morning or around mid-afternoon. With a 1, you may be very creative and get all wrapped up in yourself by focusing your concentration on your work or a hobby, which may in fact be a wonderful form of meditation because it absorbs you. When this happens you may lose yourself as a person at times because you are focusing inside your mind or connecting with your inner self so deeply. Several hours may pass by in what may seem to be a couple of minutes.

Meditation 2 With a 2, you may enjoy sharing your meditation time with somebody close to you, perhaps in the late afternoon or early evening. Meditations that help to balance your emotions may attract you, such as a musical meditation with the gentle sound of dolphins or waves of water. However, you can be dreamy at times, and sometimes, listening to soft music may mean you float off even more.

Simple exercises like focusing on your breath as it rises and falls may help to keep you centered; a few minutes may be all you need to relax.

Meditation 3 With a 3, you may like to meditate with groups of people, quite late in the evening, and you may attend different groups so that you can connect with all kinds of different people. Perhaps you find that you have psychic experiences when you meditate, such as strong instincts about people in your life. When you meditate you may take up a cross-legged position on the floor, and although simple breathing exercises may appeal you may also like to chant a mantra. One of the most common universal mantras is the word "Aum" (sounds like om), but you may prefer to use other mantras too, or may even find that one mantra is personal to you.

ABOVE Reading may put you in a meditative state of relaxation.

RIGHT Group meditation may appeal to you.

Meditation 4 With a 4, you may like to meditate where you feel secure; for example, at home or at a friend's house. Perhaps you like to meditate where you can feel your connection to the earth, in your garden, or on a bench in your local park, or simply by taking your shoes off so that you can feel your feet on the floor. Around 6pm may be your favorite time to meditate. Transcendental meditation is one method that may appeal to you because it requires practical application and perseverance. You may also like to feel physically comfortable when you are meditating.

Meditation 5 With a 5, you may find skiing a wonderful way for you to switch off and to achieve inner clarity about your life. Perhaps this occurs because you need to concentrate carefully on what you are doing, so any mind chatter simply slips away. You may also form your own meditation group and perhaps lead everyone into a meditation by reading some beautiful thoughts for the day. Sunrise may be one of your favorite times to meditate, when everything outside is fresh and clear. However, you may get easily restless with the chattering going on in the mind, and may give up on trying to meditate very easily.

Meditation 6 With a 6, you may enjoy meditating in groups because you like to see all the different aspects of yourself within them mirrored back to you, and feel that you are all a part of one world. Color meditations may appeal to you; perhaps you visualize different colors with your group, or all the different colors of the rainbow, or your chakras. You may be a very visual person, so meditating by looking at a beautiful picture or scenery may also help you to feel connected to nature. You may meditate any time, but setting aside a specific period may also help you to focus.

RIGHT Knitting is a form of relaxation and can be meditative too.

Meditation 7 With a 7, you may at times really enjoy solitude; perhaps you are a loner and enjoy sitting in a quiet spot in order to connect with your inner self and contemplate life. You may be a little dreamy by nature, and sometimes it may help if you meditate with groups of people to help you to feel connected to others too. Walking meditation, where you simply concentrate on taking small steps in front of each other may also suit. Sunrise and sunset may be two of your favorite times of the day for meditation.

Meditation 8 With an 8, you may like to meditate around midnight and midday; if this is not possible, then early evening may suffice. You may have a strong mind with a shopping list of things to do, so your mind needs to be focused inward to connect with your inner self.

Visualizations are one method to help you to meditate, such as holding the vision of a scene in your mind and concentrating on nothing else. If you meditate in groups, then it may also be a group vision you hold in your mind. Chanting a mantra silently may be a favorite way to meditate.

Meditation 9 With a 9, you may find one of the best possible ways to meditate is simply by listening to some beautiful music, like opera or classical music, or specific relaxation or New Age music. Gregorian or religious chanting may also appeal to your senses and help you to feel connected spiritually. Perhaps you like to play a musical instrument or paint and you find this a deeply satisfying way to meditate by "losing yourself," You may like to meditate in the early evening around 7pm.

ABOVE The setting sun holds beautiful qualities which may be helpful in meditation.

LEFT Choose a favorite place in which to let yourself wind down.

LEFT Soothing music can help to calm you down and uplift you spiritually.

VISUALIZATIONS

* * * * * * * * * * * * * * * * * * *

VISUALIZATION IS like painting a picture in your mind, except a visualization can be produced instantly. You take out your paints and easel, set up the scene you wish to draw and then paint it in a moment; you can also change it in a moment.

Your mind is impressionable and receptive to ideas both from the world in which you live and from your soul. A visual scene which you see in your mind may give you important information or even help to give you guidance about life. You can also influence these visualizations yourself, particularly by emotional desires and wishes, so what you see may be a projection of what you want, with no deeper message.

You may be able to work out which messages come from the soul as they may seem exceedingly simple. For example, in your mind you may see a picture of sunshine on the beach; perhaps this is giving you a message that you may need a holiday or a rest. Messages from your soul may also be about other people or situations in the world at large. You may see a picture of a peaceful ending to a conflict in a specific country. This may not be showing you that this is going to happen, but that it may be needed, and you may spend some time giving thought to a positive outcome if you choose.

Taking time out from your busy life to spend on a visualization may also help to relax you and clear your mind of clutter, and therefore help you to achieve clarity. Visualization time may be like a meditation to help to connect you to your inner self and your spirituality. You can also participate in group visualizations, which may benefit everyone in a different way or on a different level – physical, emotional, mental, or spiritual. Work out the major numbers in your chart and then look them up below to see general trends for the type of scenes you may like to visualize in your relaxation time.

The colors for these visualizations can be chosen before you begin or simply be allowed to arise. You may like to spend a few minutes or longer on these visualizations. Each time you do this you may feel different. Sit in a comfortable chair or lie down so that you can fully relax. Relaxing in the bath is also a lovely time to close your eyes and visualize for a moment or two. A few minutes at the office or even while you are sitting on the train or bus may also be effective.

If your picture changes while you are visualizing the scene appropriate to the major number in your chart, then that's fine. You may choose to go along with your new vision, or to refocus your mind back to your original vision. You may also like to identify the number of people, objects, or colors in your visualization because these numbers carry potent messages.

RIGHT The movement of water, whether tidal or from a natural spring, can help you to reflect upon life.

ABOVE Visualizing a mountain range may impart a sense of journeying in life.

RIGHT You can also create a vizualization in your mind's eye.

1 With a 1, you may like to visualize mountains. These may represent an ambition or drive to conquer them, particularly if they are steep or treacherous. They can connect with your spirituality. It may also feel like the perfect retreat, with no or few people around.

2 With a 2, you may like to visualize water. Still waters run deep, and this may help you to delve deep into your subconscious or feel at peace with yourself. Visualizing a choppy sea may unsettle you emotionally, or may help you to get in contact with unexpressed feelings.

3 With a 3, you may visualize the sky and sunshine. You may feel the warmth of the sun's rays and it may help you to feel relaxed as will a blue sky. If the sky is hazy, then it may be taking you into the fog of confusion, which you may at that time be experiencing.

4 With a 4, you may like to visualize trees or even a whole wood. Trees may help you to feel grounded and connected to the earth. Perhaps the wood is shady, which may allow you to delve into your shadow side, or it may also give you shelter and protection from the bright daylight.

5 With a 5, you may like to visualize the snow and wind. Perhaps you picture a beautiful scene where the snow is deep, the air is crisp, and the sun or moon shines clearly overhead. You may also visualize a snow storm with the wind howling around your ears; you may feel calm in its center or feel as free as the wind.

6 With a 6, you may like to visualize a cave. Perhaps the cave reminds you of a womb, where you can feel emotionally safe and secure. Or perhaps you feel insecure because there is no warmth or comfort around you.

7 With a 7, you may like to visualize a rainbow. It may remind you of all the different colors and all the different kinds of people in the world. Perhaps one color speaks the loudest. Perhaps there are only 6 colors and so you may like to focus on them, or on the missing color.

8 With an 8, you may like to visualize a bridge. The bridge may be made of steel, so that you feel its strength or it may be made out of old rope, which is also strong but requires more effort to cross. A bridge may be mirroring transformation as it leads you from one thing to another.

9 With a 9, you may like to visualize an array of different colors, one at a time, as for you the world may be rich with diversity, and you may see 20 or 30 colors at a time. Perhaps you are in a dark mood and you visualize dark colors, or you are in a good mood and visualize bright colors.

LEFT Visualize yourself in a glade, in which the branches shade you from the natural light, and sense protection.

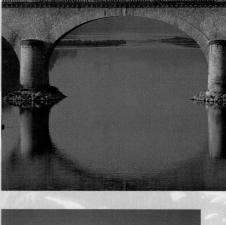

TOP Visualizations may help you realise that everything in life is linked.

ABOVE A cold landscape may help you suspend clear thoughts in your mind.

MUSIC AND SOUND

* * * * * * * * * * * * * * * *

SOUND IS VERY potent. It has the power to heal and also to destroy, the ability to uplift your mood or stir up feelings so strong that you are ready to burst. Sound Therapists use their voices to help balance the seven energy centers or chakras in the body, which in turn may help to balance your overall health.

Have you ever stopped simply to listen to the amount of different noises you are surrounded by at different times of the day? Or perhaps stopped to listen to your own breathing, your own sound rhythm? Have you also considered how your environment and the sounds in it can influence you? You may consciously choose to live in a quiet spot to get away from the masses of noisy vibrations in a busy city. Birds singing the dawn chorus can wake you up and may challenge your senses with glory and the beautiful sounds they make. Sounds also come from radio waves and from the universal switching on of computers every day. Sound carries across the world and these invisible rays pass by your door.

Everyone has their own sound and rhythm. You can become more in tune with yourself, your strengths and your shadow side, by learning more about yourself from the numbers in your chart, particularly your major numbers. In life you are learning to be yourself, to sing your own song, and let your body play its own music, so that you can listen to many other sounds, and incorpororate them into your life.

ABOVE
Momentous feelings of joy or sadness may be conveyed with a poignant piece of music.

RIGHT An infectious drum beat may reflect your own energy as a Number 1.

RIGHT Folk music may play on your heart strings during a Personal Year 6.

In this section you can look at the kinds of music that may appeal to you, which may resonate with your whole being. You can also read about the famous composer Debussy's work from his numerology chart. Let this section be music to your ears, and open up your awareness so that you can listen and hear more of life. In time you will come to realise that there are many sounds in the world, and they are all unique.

1 With a 1 in your chart or as a Personal Year Number, then you may enjoy the classics, pop music, or any music that has energy and vitality.

2 With a 2 as a Personal Year Number or in your chart, you may enjoy listening to soul music, as it helps you make contact with your deep feelings, and you may feel that this music really does reach your soul.

3 With a 3 in your chart or as a Personal Year Number, you may enjoy New Age music with its mystical sounds, as well as reggae music or classical pop.

4 With a 4 as your Personal Year Number or in your chart, you may enjoy rock music or the type of loud music you enjoy stomping around to, so that you can let your hair down.

5 With a 5 in your chart or as a Personal Year Number, you may enjoy light and uplifting music, particularly dance music because you may love to express yourself. Some light jazz music with its unpredictable sounds may also attract you.

6 With a 6 as your Personal Year Number or in your chart, you may find that music which touches your heart, such as soul or folk music with stories and ballads from the heart of a community, will appeal.

7 With a 7 as your Personal Year Number or in your chart, you may enjoy New Age music with its sounds of waterfalls, delicate vibrations, and gentle voices. You may also love music with a fineness to it, or where you can hear all the instruments playing together at once, as in some classical orchestral music.

8 With an 8 as a major number or Personal Year vibration, you may enjoy powerful music, whether that be loud pop music, dramatic classical music, or forms of dynamic Latin American music.

9 With a 9 as your Personal Year Number or in your chart, you may love to listen to tribal or ethnic music from around the world, and you may also enjoy classical music and jazz.

CLAUDE ACHILLE DEBUSSY

1862–1918

Debussy was a French composer well-known for his exotic scales and freeform music, which helped to pave the way to modern music. Debussy was renowned for his musical sensitivity and impressionism. Some of his most popular works were *Jeux*, a ballet written in 1913; the opera *La Mer* written in 1905; *Clair de Lune*, written in 1894; and *Suite Bergamasque*, written around 1890–1905.

In numerology Claude's First Name or Goal Name Number adds up to a 1, so he was a natural leader who was easily able to pave the way for others. He must have possessed a strong will and a driving ambition to create, and felt free to be himself and to find his own individuality through his music. His year of birth adds up to a 17 or 8, which highlights power, and this force was certainly directed into his work. It also influences introspection; no doubt a deep inner process of self-realization went on within him.

His Family Name Number, Debussy, was a 23 or 5, which highlights creativity, self-expression, and joy. He was also a thinker who felt deeply connected to his soul, which was expressed through his music. This number also influences the mind and the potential to delve deep into his imagination, and he may have been very perceptive too. Achille, his middle name, adds up to a 5 too, so this number, which influences dance, music, and movement, was strongly intensified in his chart. *Clair de Lune* also adds up to a 50 or a 5, and therefore his freedom to roam around (freeform style) was expressed through this simple song with its clarity of form.

As the 1 of his first name was the same number as the year of his death, perhaps he was seeking new direction at that time.

ABOVE French classical composer Claude Achille Debussy.

LEFT With an 8, you may enjoy the passionate flamenco rhythms.

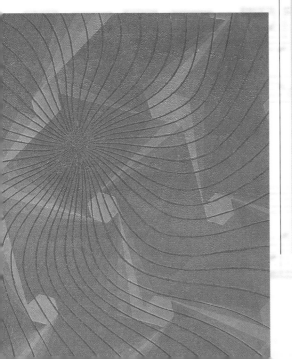

LEFT *"Magnet Force."* Music is made from the magnetism of spirit and matter.

GARDENS AND GARDENING

* * * * * * * * * * * * * * * * * *

THE NUMBERS IN your chart, particularly your major numbers, influence the number of the property you may be attracted to live in, as well as the type of garden you may have. Indeed, Numerology can help you as a guideline when redesigning your garden.

RIGHT A small, well-tended garden with carefully selected foliage and plants appeals to people with a Number 1.

Garden 1 The 1 contains the element of air, so you may like to make sure that your garden looks airy too. Perhaps you place tall trees in it, which have few branches and leaves or move very easily in the breeze. You may like to find the rarest trees, or unusual plants with their own individual feel. When designing or choosing a garden, plenty of natural light may be needed. Paths may intrigue you, and you may like to incorporate them through your garden.

ABOVE Symmetry in a garden appeals with an 8. You may work methodically and make use of all available space.

Garden 2 The 2 highlights the element of water. Perhaps you have a gentle stream or waterfall running through your garden, or a pond with water lilies floating serenely on the top. Water helps you to calm down. Gushing water in your garden, however, may stir up your emotions too much. You may also like to place two of everything in your garden: two plants of the same color or species, next to two fish ponds, or two trees. Perhaps you like jasmine when its two stems blend into one and flower together.

Garden 3 This number highlights the element of fire. Perhaps you live in a hot climate or enjoy the heat of the colors in your garden. Perhaps you literally bring fire into your garden with a barbecue or by lighting garden candles or floodlighting your garden in the evenings. Your garden may be very abundant, overflowing with flowers, bushes, and trees. It may even expand into the neighboring domain at times or look cluttered. You may prefer an open garden with no fences or walls, creating a sense of space and freedom. You may also like to create a rockery, with miniature plants peeping out here and there. Perhaps you are attracted to the idea of concrete or gravel in your garden, and to create enough space for you to sit in.

Garden 4 This number 4 highlights the element of earth, and your garden may be like Heaven on Earth to you. When you are at home you may spend more time working or enjoying your garden than you do indoors. Perhaps you even camp out in your garden, to feel your connection with the earth. Security is one of the qualities associated with this number, so you may like to have solid boundaries around your garden, perhaps planting a row of trees or surrounding it with a wooden fence. Your garden may look structured, orderly, and neat; perhaps you even plant things in squares. You may like to grow a selection of vegetables, fruits, and herbs.

Garden 5 Number 5 highlights the element of air, so you may like to feel that you can drift away in your garden. This may work literally, so you may have lots of bushes or trees to create constant movement in the breeze. Or perhaps you live at the top of a hill or on a slope. However, if you do not have trees or live near open spaces or hills, then you may like to create this sense of space, perhaps by designing a lawn with plants growing all around the edges.

You may like to design a garden with pot plants, as you may like to chop and change. Perhaps you like flowers that grow quickly. You may also love to let nature design a wild flower garden, by leaving a plot of land open for whatever blows your way in the wind.

Garden 6 The number 6 highlights the element of water, and it is a number that influences love and heart feelings. You may like to have lots of grass, trees, and greenery in your garden to help you connect with this heart energy. You may have all sorts of plants in your garden and you may take in plants that have been left for dead, bringing them to back to life under your loving care. Perhaps you also have many pretty flowers which all look jolly, or have large sensual flowers to make you feel good. You may choose plants for their smells as much as for their looks.

Garden 7 This number highlights the element of water, so you may particularly enjoy your garden at the time of the full moon, which is linked with the intuitive watery side of nature. Your garden can help to quieten your emotions, as you learn to let go through nature.

You may be a private person, so you may like to build a garden to support this. You may also build high walls, tall fences, or grow trees so that you feel protected by nature. Perhaps you like your garden to look clear, and it may have a clinical feel to it. Indeed you may have a swimming pool, natural lake, or pond in your garden.

Garden 8 This number highlights the element of earth, so you may at times feel as if you gain strength from being in your garden and connecting with the earth.

You may like to landscape your garden; you may also like to create formal gardens. You may like your garden to look rich and powerful, so you may choose trees and plants with bright red and gold leaves, or you may have enormous plants placed strategically around your garden in pots.

Garden 9 The number 9 highlights the element of fire; in your garden this may mean that you like plants, trees, and shrubs which seem to light up in the sunshine. You may be particularly responsive to the sun and you may choose plants which react accordingly.

You may also be interested in the environment or conservation, so you may help to support and encourage local animals and wildlife into your garden.

LEFT Number 2; Plants that grow entwined may signify the interconnection of life.

LEFT Number 4; you may like your garden to look orderly and neat.

FENG SHUI

* * * * * * * * * * * * * * * * * * *

FENG SHUI IS the ancient art of placement used in China for many thousands of years. It is now very popular in the West. All objects are made up of energy, and there is a relationship between the position of objects in your home, office, or garden, and the lessons you need to learn in life. When feng shui is applied with numerology it becomes an extremely potent tool, because it highlights areas where energies are flowing or where there may be energy blocks. This can be seen using traditional feng shui methods and also by observing the numbers in your chart, particularly your major numbers and your specific Personal Year Number. Each corner of your room represents a compass point, for example, north, northeast, east, southeast – and each of these directions is associated with a number, forming a map.

ABOVE A compass helps you to see in which direction you are facing.

In feng shui you take this map and superimpose it onto a map or drawing of your home or office, and then onto each individual room within your home, and also gardens and balconies if you choose, identifying the layout with the relevant compass points. Then you can take the major numbers in your chart and correspond them with the map, to observe areas of personal development and therefore physical areas within your property that may need particular attention. For example, if your Life Path Number is a 51/6, then Area 6, which relates to family, is highlighted in terms of the collective group needs, and you are particularly learning lessons in life associated with this. "Family" includes the family you were born into, your partner, children, and also all your ancestors. If Area 6 faces southwest in your home, for example, you may wish to place pictures of your family in this area. It is interesting to see what is already there. For example, you may have dirty old boots, or your accounts books in Area 6. What you store in these areas may already give you a clue as to the way in which you may view these relationships.

It is also interesting to see the shape of the objects in a particular space or room. Again, for example, if you have sharp objects in your family area 6, then subconsciously you may have placed them there because currently there may be aggression and hostility among your own family household members, or within extended family relationships. You may wish to change this by placing other objects there to help improve family relationships.

Objects are divided into two groups: yin or rounded objects; and yang or sharp objects; some objects can be a mixture of both. In numerology yin represents the even numbers 2, 4, 6, and 8 and highlights shadow or darkness. Yang represents the odd numbers 1, 3, 5, 7,

THE FENG SHUI NUMEROLOGY MAP

NW
Wealth

N
Fame, Popularity, Recognition

NE
Love and Relationships

1
8   2
9
W   7   GENERAL   3   **E**
Career/Work   HEALTH   *Play*
6   4
5

Family
SW

Creativity
S

Friends
SE

and 9 and highlights light. You may notice that, if you have lots of odd numbers in your chart, like 7s or 9s, then you may place many sharp objects in your home or, paradoxically, you may wish to incorporate polar opposites by placing round objects there to complement your environment.

Life is a constant balancing act and in an ideal world you are working toward finding equilibrium in your environment. At times you may seem to go out of balance, and perhaps your home represents this by having an over-abundance of yin or yang objects within it, and by having too much light or darkness, or light or dark colors. These may, however, denote a time essential for transformation and growth; when things are changing, even for the better, they go out of balance for a while, then restore themselves, until the whole process starts again.

What may feel right for you to place in your home or work environment at one point in your life may not feel right later on. Having objects around you that are out of balance may at times help you to go in deeply into the lessons associated with the numbers and areas to which they correspond. You may be able to help the balancing process along if you choose to observe the numbers in your chart and balance out the placement of objects within it, too. Indeed fresh air, sunlight, and a clutter-free environment may all help your life to flow.

In feng shui numerology, by observing your Personal Year Number during a specific year, you can see which issues may arise during that time, and in what area of your life. Your Personal Year Number can also help to bring out the energies associated with that area, particularly if it is in your chart already. For example, if you are currently influenced by a 4 Personal Year, and you have a Karma Number 4, then it can help to enhance your friendships as the number 4 relates to the friends area. Perhaps your relationships deepen or you become more secure with your friends, or perhaps you find that some friend becomes a major challenge to you. When you are influenced by a Personal Year Number, as with the number 4 in the above example, it does not mean that every other area of your chart is excluded from your life during that specific year. If you are influenced by a 4, then you can build on your friendships within your work, play, and intimate life.

The same applies to your major numbers; even if some numbers don't show up in the Feng Shui Numerology Key, you still relate to all those areas of your life. Your major numbers give you guidelines as to some of the significant areas you may be working with in your life.

LEFT The combination of feng shui with numerology can be very potent.

BELOW Planning your home around the principles of feng shui can be very rewarding.

MISSING AREAS

The overall shape of your home may not look like a complete square as in the feng shui numerology key, and you may indeed have bits "missing." You may live in an oblong building, or a round house, so areas may be absent when you figure out your feng shui map. These are helpful tools to help you with your personal development and your whole life, because they are little clues as to what issues you may be currently working with and therefore lessons you may need to learn. If you are a newly-wed and have just moved into a new home and discover that your love and relationship area – 2, northeast – is missing, then this means you may need to work on this. Perhaps one or both of you have the Number 2 in your chart already, or you are in a 2 Personal Year. You can also use some basic feng shui tools such as crystals, plants, or marriage photographs (in this case), and place them in your home to help enhance your relationship together. Perhaps your relationship is the main focus of attention in your home.

With feng shui numerology it is possible for you to enter a property and literally read it like an open book, identifying areas that are moving or others that are stagnant, and working out which part of life they apply to for the people living or working there. If you work from home, then operating from the work area 7 may help to enhance your career. You can also read information from the number of the property, particularly if you have your property number existing in your chart already. It can also help to bring out the qualities associated with that number, even if it is not in your chart.

ABOVE Natural crystals represent the mineral kingdom and can help to enhance your environment.

Sometimes many numbers may influence your property or office. For example, Apartment 901, at 68 Green Lane, has the numbers 9, 1, 6, and 8 influencing it, as well as the sum total of those numbers together: $9 + 1 + 6 + 8 = 24$, $2 + 4 = 6$. This final digit between 1 to 9 generally has the strongest influence over your whole life for as long as you are living there. The number can also highlight the types of work you may carry out while you are working there. With a 6 you may work as a graphic artist, or a doctor.

NUMBERS, ELEMENTS, AND LESSONS

1 With a 1 in your chart or as a Personal Year number, you have the element of air influencing you, so you may like to bring in fresh air into your life or to take a good look at the direction where you are heading. As this is the fame or popularity area, then you may be learning to find your own individuality and to be yourself. When you feel comfortable in your own skin, this shines through and you may be very popular. Hanging mobiles about your home may help you to keep the energy moving.

2 With a 2 as a Personal Year Number or major number, you are influenced by the element of water. Perhaps water is a major feature in your home or in your garden, or your shower room is one of your favorite areas where you spend a lot of time. The 2 is associated with the love and relationships area, so you are learning to share yourself, to open up to love and allow yourself to connect emotionally, and to learn to relate to others in a loving way. Placing pairs of things in this area, which represent balance, may help your relationships too.

3 With a 3 as a Personal Year Number or major number vibration, you are influenced by the element of fire. Indeed, you may pay particular attention to the lighting in terms of your needs. This 3 area is called the play area because 3 is associated with play, fun, joy, and relaxation. Indeed, this may be one area of your property where you like to sit.

4 With a 4 as a major number or Personal Year vibration, you are influenced by the element of earth. You may like to feel the earth beneath your feet and you may literally walk around the property barefoot, perhaps on wooden floors. This is the friends area, so loyalty and friendship may be important to you. One of your lessons may be to help bring stability into your life by forming strong bonds of friendships with other people.

5 With a 5 as a Personal Year Number or major number, you are influenced by the element of air. You may like your environment to feel light and airy. This is the creativity area and painting it light colors, or hanging up windchimes help keep the atmosphere clear.

6 With a 6 as a major number or Personal Year Number, you are influenced by the element of water, so may have a water feature. It is associated with sensitivity. Number 6 can also help to bring out a sensual feel to the esthetics. This 6 area is associated with Family, and you may need to learn to consider your whole family's needs.

7 With a 7 as a Personal Year Number or major number, you are influenced by the element of water, so you may enjoy pale pastel colors, which may enhance your ability to comunicate in life. This is the career area, and one of the qualities of the 7 is productivity. You may feel happiest when you are able to get things together and to produce things. One of your lessons is to be realistic about your career.

8 With an 8 as your Personal Year Number or as a major number, you are influenced by the element of earth. You may like to have lots of woody plants around, perhaps money plants to bring their energy into your property. The 8 area is associated with wealth. One of your lessons is to learn to value your inner spiritual connection as much as your material possessions.

9 With a 9 as a major number or Personal Year vibration, you are influenced by the element of fire. Perhaps you place lots of bright candles around your property or paint it in bright passionate colors. Area Number 9 is called the general area and keeping this area physically clear can help all the other areas of your property and your life to flow too. One lesson may be to learn to discriminate about what you want or need in life.

LEFT Number 5; windchimes are free to move around, and help keep things flowing.

BELOW Number 8; a money plant may give you joy, and help bring positive energy into your life.

PART FOUR

COMMUNICATION AND WORK

★ ★ ★ ★ ★

Communication is needed in order to be understood and you are constantly communicating to the world in many different ways; by verbal communication and body language, and through art, religion, culture, and so on. These subjects are explored with numerology. Indeed, numerology can help explain why certain people may have difficulty understanding each other and point at areas of possible communication.

The numbers in your chart, most importantly, the Personal Year Cycles 1–9, highlight potential trends which can influence you in your work or field, and can also influence you to take up a specific focus on your career path.

Through the ages, patterns have emerged, and the nature of events – whether they have been political, economic, or humanitarian – has raised significant issues and lessons; in turn, these have shaped the whole of humanity.

ABOVE Communication is vital for everyday living.

COMMUNICATION SKILLS

* * * * * * * * * * * * * * * * * *

LEFT For American philosopher John Searle, an investigation of language is an investigation of the structure of experience.

LIFE IS CONTINUALLY communicating to you and everything else on this planet, and you may pick up and interpret many of its messages on a subconscious level. On a personal level the nervous system in your body is continually communicating between your brain and different parts of your body, although you are not consciously aware of this. Communication can also take place on any of the four levels – physical, emotional, mental, and spiritual – and signals are given out and received at different times and in different ways. Communication is therefore a complex business.

Words in themselves are worthless. The energy you give them and the thoughts and feelings behind them are what have an effect. For example, you may ask your partner, "Can you order a pizza for brunch?" in a gentle way, or in an angry manner. Your tone of voice can reveal a hidden agenda that you may or may not be aware of. Sometimes you may ask for something politely, but the person receiving the communication may take it another way because of the way their mind, body, and spirit are functioning at that moment in time.

ABOVE On the telephone, it is possible to convey powerful messages through your tone of voice, and the intention of what you want to say.

Numerology can teach more about the ways in which you communicate by looking at the qualities contained within the potential of the major numbers in your chart. It may help you to make the most out of your potential in life. For example, with a 5 Personality Number, you may make a good public speaker or have a fear of speaking out, because this is one of the numbers which is specifically associated with self-expression and communication. Numerology can also teach you more about the person with whom you are communicating. It also gives them clues about methods of communication so as to help them be more open and responsive toward you.

1 With a 1, you may be learning to be direct in your communication and to be clear about what you need to say to people. This may be particularly the case in relationships where intimacy is concerned, as you may sometimes be detached about what you are saying. You may like to hear your voice raised over everyone else's at times; you may sometimes even seem bullish and strident. You may communicate to others through the exchange of thoughts and ideas.

2 With a 2, you may express how you feel, and discuss your feelings about life in general with others. This may allow people to get emotionally close, which may encourage them to open up their feelings. Sometimes your feelings may be given too much significance, though, and you may miss the facts within a situation.

3 With a 3, you may like to communicate with others by singing to them or by chatting with them. Perhaps you flit from one subject to another and like to keep the tempo light and upbeat. You may also communicate through touch.

4 With a 4, you may like to communicate through physical actions; perhaps you use your hands and arms to gesture. You may generally think carefully about what you want to

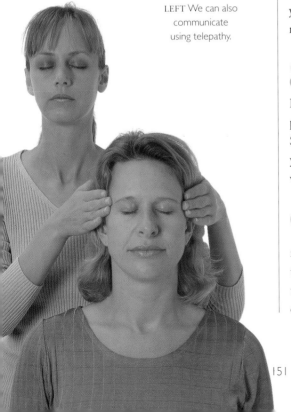

LEFT We can also communicate using telepathy.

say, because you like to keep your word.

5 With a 5, you may like to communicate through writing and you understand the responsibility of the words you use within your speech. Perhaps you like to be as factual as possible, although you may sometimes be dismissive and sceptical about what others have to say.

6 With a 6, you may be very aware of how you dress each day, because you like to look good. Sometimes you may also judge a situation by looks alone, which may mean that you do not pick up true communication. At times you may also follow your "gut feelings" about what to communicate.

7 With a 7, you may be detached at times, which may mean that you seem to communicate in a blunt manner. Sometimes you may be unaware of what you are saying because you may be dreamy or thinking deeply. You may communicate telepathically.

8 With an 8, your thoughts give you a clue as to how to communicate with others. Perhaps you take a passive approach to some people, and an assertive approach toothers. Sometimes you may blurt out what you think you want to say rather than paying attention to what you really need to be communicating.

9 With a 9, you may be able to communicate and get along with anyone, as you may be completely flexible to whatever situation arises. Perhaps you like to fit into life and to be accepted by those around you, or feel that everyone can teach you something special.

LEFT Instant communication via the Internet may suit people with a Number 5.

EDUCATION AND LEARNING SKILLS

* * * * * * * * * * * * * * * * * * *

FROM THE MOMENT you are born – and even inside the womb – you are constantly learning about life. You only need to observe toddlers to see how they hold or look at every new thing with wonder. This fascination for learning continues subconsciously through all your life on a soul level, and on the personality level you may be more consciously aware of the things life continues to teach you.

RIGHT Teaching life skills through play begins at an early age.

Everyone has their own different ways of learning, which are explored in this section, but we all have something in common in that we all learn through experience. Only by burning your fingers on hot toast, for example, do you learn to let it cool down a little before you pick it up next time. It is also human nature to forget things; if you have not eaten toast for 20 years you may forget what to do. Lessons keep coming back in life for you to be able to refine them, so that through this experience you really understand what you need to learn.

BELOW Number 6 children are stimulated to learn subjects with a highly visual impact.

To find out more about your potential learning characteristics, work out your Personality Number from your day of birth, highlighting your psychological patterns of behavior. You can also learn important lessons from your past experiences which are highlighted in other numbers in your chart, such as your Soul Number.

RIGHT Number 4; if you take an audio-visual course, you can do it at your own pace, step by step.

HOW DO YOU LEARN?

1 With a 1, you may have a good memory or have trained your mind to remember things from an early age, perhaps by associating words with things that then stick in your mind. You may also learn through concepts and ideas, either your own or others. Perhaps you are very bright and like to show off. At times you may feel defeated if you cannot grasp a subject, but this can also teach you something.

2 With a 2, you may be very impressionable and open to life, so you may absorb knowledge easily. You may particularly learn through your feelings, and if you feel as if you can relate to someone you may learn more easily. Listening is an essential quality, which you may need to learn with this number 2; listening to audio teaching tools may help you. Listening to others' wisdom about life may be enjoyable. Your fear of rejection may prevent you from learning at times.

3 With a 3, you may love to learn. Humor may be one way to ensure that a subject keeps your attention when you are learning something new. You may like to doodle amusing images when people are talking to you. Drawing pictures and writing things down, expressing what you are learning, may

152

help you to remember things more easily. You may be easily distracted and get bored with learning.

4 With a 4, you may learn through application and routine, as you really like to experience life practically. Perhaps you like to learn in a systematic way, little by little, with everything laid out and well planned in advance. Structured learning times may help you to feel secure as you know what you will be learning next. When life doesn't go to plan (as is life's habit!), then you may really struggle with what you may need to learn and resist the process.

5 With a 5, you may enjoy learning through verbal exchange and communication and be able to ask lots of questions and discuss the answers you receive. You may also like the freedom to be able to explore what you are learning and to think things through. You may like to experiment by learning about different types of subjects. Sometimes you may restrict yourself to focus on one thing, and your mind may get stuck on this.

6 With a 6, you find that one sound way for you to learn is through enjoyment and pleasure. If a subject does not make you feel good, then you may drop it altogether. Visuals may help you learn, such as a beautiful cookbook if you are in a cookery class, and so on. You may also enjoy learning by either helping or supporting others with their learning process. Perhaps your instincts guide you to those subjects and lessons which you need to learn in life.

7 With a 7, you may be a fast learner and pick up things at the drop of a hat. You may have masterminded a computer literally overnight. Your intuition and your powers of observation may also help you to make the most of any subject you are learning about. At times you may be impatient, and this may hamper your learning abilities. You may also agonize over information, which can slow down the learning process.

8 With an 8, you may find that others' success in education spurs you on to try harder and achieve more. You may like to lead the way in whichever subjects you choose, and give 100 percent. You may have an intellectual mind, so books may be good tools for you to use. Fear of failure, or of doing well, may prevent you from learning a subject.

9 With a 9, you may learn easily when you are inspired by people, and so you may choose your teachers carefully. Perhaps you may own a library full of biographies that can enrich your life, and perhaps you aspire to emulate the achievements of these subjects. You may also have your own store of inner knowledge, which comes from your inner wisdom from the past. You may not learn because you insist that you are always right – in which case there is nothing more that you can learn!

LEFT Number 7; computers can provide huge amounts of information, suitable for fast learners.

LEFT You may learn about life from your own special library of books.

BODY LANGUAGE

* * * * * * * * * * * * * * * * * * * *

BODY LANGUAGE DESCRIBES the way that your body communicates messages from the way you stand, sit, talk, look, and move. Each person interprets these messages in their own way, according to their own individual make-up. If you live in Australia, where there is lots of space in relation to the amount of people who live there, then you may stand some distance away from people when you first meet.

In a big city like London, if you meet someone and talk to them from a similar distance they may regard you as unfriendly because you are placing space between yourself and them. However, if you were to study body language around the world you would find that the general meanings of basic common movements are the same.

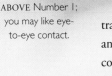

ABOVE Number 1; you may like eye-to-eye contact.

Body language is very useful when you are traveling or interacting with different people in any kind of situation because it can help you to communicate what you need to say, as well as guide you to an understanding of what is happening. You may have stepped off an aeroplane in some foreign land and, although you did not understand the language, you might have had an immediate feel for the culture. This happens even with your first impression in the first few minutes, as you subconsciously weigh up the way in which people you see, meet, or interact with, are standing, sitting or talking.

Your body language may differ when you are with a lover or when you are with a business partner or a child. How you both interact can be observed from the numbers in your chart. Add up the major numbers of your chart and your Personal Year number, and see some of the potential traits associated with each one. You incorporate many different movements and gestures at once, but general trends may apply.

RIGHT Number 2; folding your arms indicates you may be feeling uncomfortable or are being defensive.

1 With a 1, you may be a person who likes to be direct in your dealings with others and in life, so you may like to use eye-to-eye contact as much as possible. If you fear intimacy, then you may shy away from eye contact. Other stances you may take are to clench your hands together as you sit at a table or to place them in front of you on your lap, highlighting a tense and uptight feeling. You may be feeling frustrated with the person you are speaking to or have a more general dissatisfaction with life.

2 With a 2, you may like to meet people in the middle and feel equal, so you may enjoy shaking hands, which can signify a coming together and a meeting ground. You may also be fearful and doubt yourself; at these times you may place your hand over your mouth. Another common body language gesture with the influence of the 2 may be that you cross your hands in a defensive way, perhaps to keep people away because you are feeling vulnerable.

3 With a 3, you are learning how to express yourself more successfully through verbal communication and creativity, so you may adopt the gesture of lip-biting, as you bite back what you have to express. Sometimes you may also find yourself rubbing your ears when you don't want to hear what others are saying to you or about you.

4 With a 4, you like to feel secure in your environment and comfortable with your company in whatever circumstances, so you may adopt the gesture of standing a good distance away from people you first meet, until you can feel safe with them. You may also be secretive at times, and this may be mirrored with the stance of hands tucked into your two back pockets.

5 With a 5, you may like movement; you may be restless at times. You are also learning to communicate as one of your lessons, so the gesture of rubbing the palms of your hands together may be one of the movements associated with this number, which communicates a desire to move on. You may also be dismissive of others' communication at times, which is mirrored as you make an arch with your hands, with your fingers touching.

6 With a 6, you are influenced a great deal by your feelings and emotions, so you may adopt the stance of holding your own hands, particularly in front of you to help you to feel supported and secure. At other times you may place your fingers in your mouth to give yourself reassurance. Babies often do this as it is very comforting and nurturing. If you feel emotionally insecure, then this is another reason why you may make this gesture.

7 With a 7, you are learning to trust yourself and others, and you may use your intuition to help guide you at times. You may therefore adopt the stance of wrapping both of your hands around people's hands in a handshake when you meet them, particularly if you are familiar with them already, in order to communicate your trust. When you feel safe with people, you may also make the gesture of opening your palms to them, which is revealing the inner you.

8 With an 8, you may like to show that you are strong, powerful, and in control of your life, so you may often adopt the gesture of thumbs up, which communicates that you are in control of the situation in which you find yourself. Indeed, if you are okay, then others must be okay too, because you're the boss! Sometimes you may also make a gesture of gripping your wrist firmly with your other hand behind your back, because it may help you to maintain or regain your self-control.

9 With a 9, you may like to educate yourself in many different areas of general knowledge. At times when you are in situations where you don't understand, you may make the gesture of shrugging your shoulders, as you think, "uhh?" You can also be highly opinionated and feel superior to others, so you may talk to them with your chin pointed down in a critical way, so that it looks as though they are peering up to you, and you are looking down on them in a superior fashion.

ABOVE Number 8; you may like to give people the thumbs up – "OK".

LEFT Public speakers communicate a great deal through body language.

ABOVE Number 4; Hiding hands in the pocket may reveal a secretive nature.

LEFT Number 6; you may be trying to get to grips with your emotions.

DEVELOPING YOUR CAREER

* * * * * * * * * * * * * * * * * * *

YOU HAVE GIFTS, talents, and interests associated with each of the major numbers in your chart. With a 4 Personality, you may work as an accountant; your Life Path Number may be 7, which means that you may take up a career where you work with your intuition. Your Soul and Karma Numbers may also be different and highlight other potential career paths that you may like to follow.

In an ideal world you would use all your talents. If you were an accountant by day, you might occasionally work as a healer in the evenings. You would also bring all the qualities together into one job or one career. In this instance, you would use your intuition when doing a company's book-keeping to find the best way to sort out their accounts. In this world you would also choose to focus on one particular career or talent when it is highlighted in a specific Personal Year.

Work out your major numbers – your Personality, Life Path, Soul, Childhood, Karma, and Personal Year Numbers – then look up the general trends associated within their potential and for each specific year.

Numbers at Work

1 You may work in an area where you can use your inventive mind to create original ideas; you may become a leader. If you work for a business, you may achieve leadership status as a result of your creative input. You may also like to join a company which leads a particular field so that you are certain about your goals, focus, and direction. You may be a public relations expert, a designer, public figure, an inventor or pioneer.

2 With a 2, you may be working in a career where you feel supported, particularly emotionally, or where you can support others; you may be a nurse, a doctor, a carer, or a social worker. You may also like to work in a profession where fairness and equality rule, such as in the legal profession, or you may even consider a career as a politician or a diplomat, where you can spend your time measuring up both sides and making decisions to bring balance to any situation. With a 2, you may also be a professional swimmer, as water is associated with your emotions.

3 With a 3, you may have taken up a career where you can sing, dance, act, or be on stage as an entertainer, because you revel in the glare of the spotlight and love being the centre of attention, and may have a gift to be able to inspire others. Perhaps you may also work as a writer or an artist, as the 3 highlights the potential of being gifted with your hands, or you may be a hairdresser, chef, or massage therapist, where your "healing hands" come into play. You may also have chosen a career where you can use your mind, because you may enjoy mental stimulation, or you may have become a social secretary.

ABOVE Number 4; you may be practical with numbers, and attracted to a career in accountancy or book-keeping.

RIGHT With water as a key element of the Number 2, you may even take up a career as swimmer.

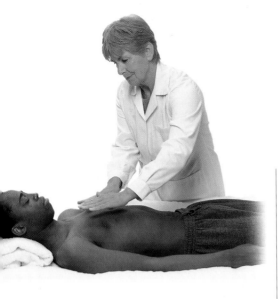

Perhaps you work as a fashion model. Any area of the medical profession may appeal, or a career in the legal field.

7 With a 7, you may have a wonderful gift to be able to produce things and make things happen, so you may take up a career as a film producer, a personal assistant (to someone high-powered), or as an adminstrator, or find yourself in any position needing organizational skills. You may also work as a healer, a complementary therapist, a psychotherapist, or in an area where you can develop and use your intuition to help others.

LEFT Number 7; a career as a therapist may appeal.

4 With a 4 in your chart, you may take up a career as an accountant, book-keeper, numerologist, or statistician, in areas where your love of numbers can be put to practical use. You may work as a gardener or farmer so that you can maintain your contact with the earth, or as a maintenance engineer or builder so that you use your practical gifts. You may also work as a household help, to learn more about responsibility.

5 With a 5, you may work as a scientist or as an inventor; you may have a brilliant mind. With your zest for adventure, you may also work in any area of the travel industry, and your magnetic nature may mean that you have great fun. You may also enjoy working in public relations or a people-related industry. You may also become a translator.

6 With a 6 in your chart, you may be interested in working with children, perhaps as a nanny, a nursery nurse, a children's counselor, or in the field of Social Services. You may be very creative artistically, and therefore work as a designer of pottery, clothes, or furniture, which is very visually stimulating.

8 With an 8, you may like to lead, so you may become an entrepreneur, guiding your own company and working as your own boss, standing up on your own two feet. Or you may work for a company that encourages you to take on responsibility and power, or even one that offers you some kind of public status so that you receive external recognition for your work. Perhaps you are the managing director, or you have a senior position in your department.

9 With an 9, you may work as a teacher or in any position within the field of education, because you may love to learn and value the knowledge you can then pass on to others. You may also be artistic, or perhaps you are a professional musician, dancer, or writer. Politics and religion may also appeal and you may take up a post where you can serve your community, or campaign for people's rights.

LEFT Numerology can help you when you are starting out on your career.

MANAGEMENT AND HUMAN RESOURCES

* * * * * * * * * * * * * * * * * *

NUMEROLOGY IS AN essential tool when it comes to recruitment. It can help you to find the best possible staff for a role, bringing together the best possible team and helping you to understand staff problems and work more efficiently. Time is money in business, and numerology can help to highlight potential strengths and challenges before they become problems.

This section of the book illustrates some of the influential trends associated with the numbers 1 to 9. Work out the major numbers in your chart, and also your Personal Year Number, and then look them up below.

You can also add up the full name of the company you own or work for, to see its numerological influences.

VISION

Everyone needs a vision, whether short- or long-term. The clearer your vision, the more you may achieve, because this sends clear messages of intention out to the world. When you work with a company, or within a department, or with a client, usually their vision will match your own to some degree. You may work for a company with no vision for itself or the team, which may be challenging. Your vision can also

RIGHT Global enterprises arise from people sharing the same vision.

change, which is why you may choose to pursue new work or a new job. Look particularly at your Life Path Numbers to highlight these trends.

1 Your vision may be to help create one world, and it may be important for people who work with you to share the same vision.

2 Your vision may be to help create harmony in the world, and you may like to work in a peaceful setting with caring people.

3 Your vision may be to help create a world full of joy, and you may bring your enthusiasm for life into your work.

4 Your vision may be to help create a world that is secure and safe, and you may like to feel comfortable in any work situation.

5 Your vision may be to help create a world where everyone has freedom of speech, and perhaps you follow this principle at work.

6 Your vision may be to help create a world that involves everyone in the picture, and at work you may recognize the role of everyone in the group.

7 Your vision may be to help create spiritual awareness in the world, and at work you may enable others to feel spiritually connected.

8 Your vision may be to help create a world where money and inner wealth go hand in hand; at work you may lead in this direction.

9 Your vision may be to help create a liberated world, and at work you may feel free to be yourself and to express your individuality.

VALUES

Your own personal values do not have to match those of the company you work for completely, but if you work along the same lines, then it can ultimately help you all to be more successful. When you are true to yourself, you set up a resonance that draws other like-minded people to you. Pay particular attention to your Soul and Karma Numbers when looking at the influences here.

1 You may value independence at work.
2 You may value co-operation at work.
3 You may value humor at work.
4 You may value responsibility at work.
5 You may value communication at work.
6 You may value team participation at work.
7 You may value space at work.
8 You may value leadership at work.
9 You may value education at work.

ABOVE A sense of responsibility is vital to your work.

LEFT Your working behavior may be infused with humor.

FAR LEFT You value communication among your colleagues.

ABOVE With a 5, you use communication to solve problems.

SKILLS

Your individual skills need to match those required for a particular role, and you may have many different ones you can utilize throughout your career. Listed here are skills which you may possess in relation to problem-solving. To highlight the trends that could potentially be influencing you, look at all the major numbers in your chart.

1 You may be a wonderful problem-solver because you have a head full of ideas, but at times they may float around in your head and you may not get around to pinning them down or materializing them.

2 You may find that you make decisions about problem-solving from your gut instincts, but sometimes your feelings can cloud the situation and may get in the way of what is needed.

3 You may have a positive outlook to problem-solving and be flexible to trying different things, but sometimes your solutions may cause more chaos.

4 You may be brilliant at coming up with practical solutions to solve problems, but you may also become an ostrich at times and resist facing them.

RIGHT Number 4; you may solve problems in a practical, efficient way.

5 You may like to be as factual as possible in order to help you to solve problems that may require a certain amount of communication. You may sometimes procrastinate.

6 You may feel a sense of duty about helping to solve problems for everyone around you, but at times you may solve your own problems first to make sure you feel okay.

7 You may use your intuition or your creative imagination to help you to solve problems, but at times you may lose your grip on reality and panic.

8 You may be able to see the end results of a problem and also see the solution at the same time, but sometimes you can be stubborn and think that only your solution is right.

9 You may use your common sense and logical brain to help you to solve problems, but sometimes problems mount up because you are too relaxed about them.

CAREER DEVELOPMENT AND NUMEROLOGY

Numerology can help you to identify the areas of your work in which you best communicate, as well as teaching you how to understand your challenging areas. It can also be a useful tool if you are preparing for a new job, considering a complete career change, or seeking promotion. In numerology, your Personality Number influences your psychological patterns of behavior, and your Life Path Number influences your greater goal. These numbers can help guide you to make the most of your potential on your career path.

FAR LEFT
Communicating through training helps build strong career foundations.

LEFT A flexible approach may open up new work opportunities.

BELOW LEFT
Curbing your panic will help you problem-solve more clearly.

BELOW Demanding careers may enrich your natural ability to follow ideas through.

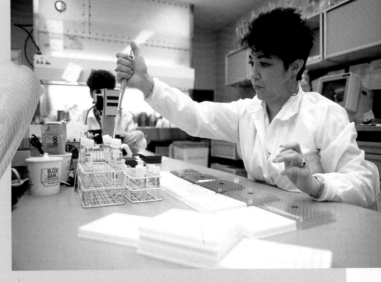

THE BUSINESS WORLD

****

NUMEROLOGY CAN HELP you to make the most out of your career in every area of the business world. Perhaps you own your own company and wish to find out more about its potential, or want more information about other companies you work with in order to highlight areas of compatibility, like making comparisons with a relationships chart.

Numerology also highlights timing in business from the Universal Personal Year, Month, Week, and Daily Cycles, so you can find some of the best potential times to launch products, sign contracts, hold business meetings or conferences, or make travel arrangements. It does not do this in a predictive way because life always throws up unforeseen or unexpected events that may make you change your path or may be just take a detour.

This section indicates some key areas of business numerology.

RIGHT Different currencies bring different number energies to trade with.

THE STOCK EXCHANGE

The London Stock Exchange is one of the largest in the world and was first set up in 1802, which adds up to a 11/2. This number 11 highlights dynamism, vitality, goal-setting, and inspiration, but it is also a nervous and unpredictable energy at times. The number 2, however, influences exchange and balance, which is constantly trying to be achieved in relation to fixing a price for shares; demand for shares should relate to the supply.

GLOBAL TRADING

If you are trading in certain currencies, then you can check the current date to see which currencies are highlighted. For example, if today's date is 14th July 2000, which adds up to a 23/5, then currencies that add up to 5 are significant. This means that they may possibly be trading well or that they become unpre-

RIGHT The stock market rises and falls according to the energy number vibration influencing that day.

RIGHT Changing your company name or building can prove to be profitable.

ABOVE Currencies have powerful symbols, too.

dictable (another quality of the 5). Perhaps the name of the company on whose behalf you are trading or the product you are trading in also adds up to a 5, which may intensify the situation or make it potentially compatible.

CURRENCIES

To work out the number of a currency, simply translate each letter into a number (A = 1, B = 2, and so on) and then add these up to form a single digit.

1	PESO, RUPIAH
2	DEUTSCHE MARK
3	PESETA, SCHILLING
4	BAHT, LIRA, ESCUDO
5	YEN, STERLING
6	FRANC, GUILDER
7	WON
8	DOLLAR
9	HONG KONG DOLLAR, KRONE

COMPANY NAMES

Numerology can help you choose the best possible company name. A suitable name is usually one containing numbers associated with the kind of work you carry out. For example, if you have a communications company, then you may wish to incorporate a name that adds up to a 3 or 5 or one that has lots of these numbers contained within it. If you own a pharmacy company then names with a 6, which highlights medicine, may also be ideal; a building company, may need to have lots of 4s or 8s or have 4 or 8 letters in its name.

Numbers which are also in your personal Numerology chart, particularly as major numbers, influence the kind of career or business you may work in. Particularly if you own the company, these numbers may need to be incorporated into the name of the company too. For example, if your Life Path Number is a 25/7 and you wish to set up a market research company, then you may like to include the 7 (which highlights research and technical detail) and 5 (influencing communication) within your company name.

RIGHT Merging companies can benefit from the different energies they inherit from the partnership.

BELOW Observing your Personal and Universal Year Cycles can help you find the best product name, design, and timing for its launch.

PRODUCT NAMING

The same process applies to product naming as to company naming. It helps to match up your market with the name of your product, and numerology can help. Timing is also important and by observing Universal Year Cycles you can understand more about potential product trends during any specific year.

BUSINESS PROPERTY AND TELEPHONE NUMBERS

It goes without saying that these are of the utmost significance as they are the first way for people to contact or perhaps work with you.

Add up the names of the building and also the departmental names within your building.

MERGING COMPANIES

Merging companies is like getting married if you merge both your names together. You keep the influence of your original names, but you also take on different energies from your joint partnership. You may merge because you can help each other build a better business together, or offer customers a better service or generally to make more money. When you merge you have both taken on additional lessons to teach each other, seen in the numbers in your joint chart.

The date that a company registers or starts trading is its birth date; the date of the merger is your joint birth date. It's interesting to examine any official documentation at the time, to obtain further clues about the issues you may be working on together. Your company registration number (both separately and together), can also have an influence over your business life.

RECRUITMENT

Whether you are simply working with someone on a short project or intending to set up a long-term business with them, Numerology can help to highlight areas of compatibility and identify potential conflicts. Sometimes this can save you all a great deal of time and money.

If you are employing staff, numerology can highlight specific skills and personal qualities essential to that job. It can also help to match the company's needs with the employees' needs, therefore creating a potentially ideal place in which to work.

feel that she may be unsettled and restless and perhaps not be able to make the commitment (potential qualities of the 5). They may take this into account, but at the end of the day nothing in life is 100 percent certain and they may take the risk on her. Awareness of this circumstance at least helps you to deal with challenges before they become problems.

BELOW Team commitment is vital in any business venture for achieving the best results.

TEAM BUILDING

Numerology can also help as a personal development tool for team building, so that the members of a whole company or group can see the part they play within the whole team, as well as their strengths and challenges within that team. It can also help to focus the group on a specific project together.

When recruiting with Numerology, even at times when the company and the employee are matched, the Personal Year Cycles may highlight potential incompatibilities. For example, an Artist may apply for a job for which she seems ideal, but her prospective employer is looking for someone long-term. As she is currently influenced by a 5 Personal Year, they may

LEFT Recruiting is a skilled business, and numerology may assist you in finding the ideal candidate.

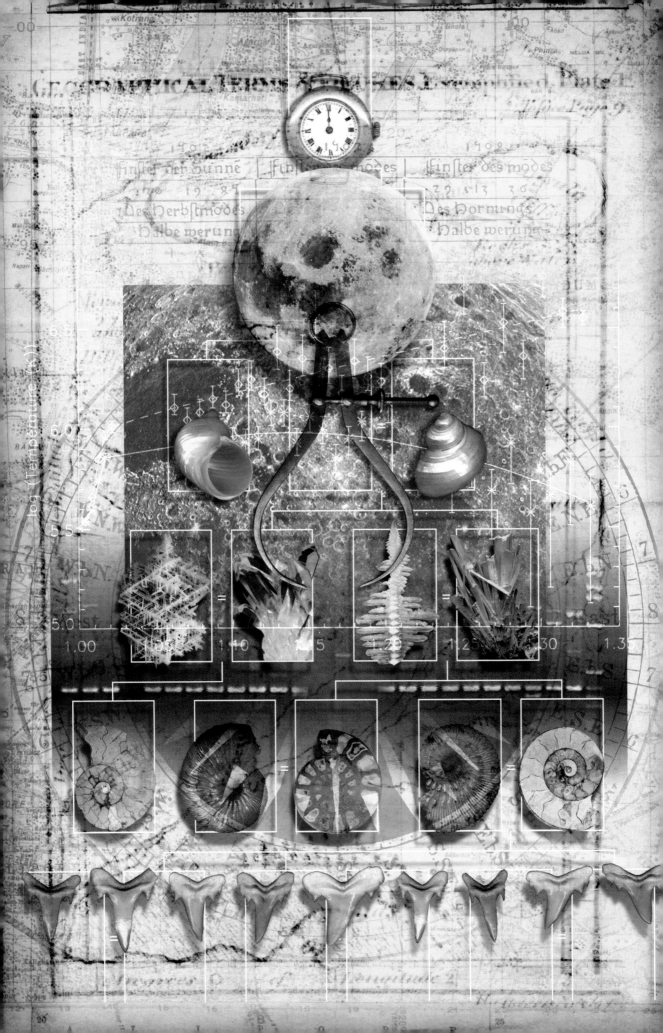

PART FIVE

The Bigger Picture

★ ★ ★ ★ ★

You are consciously or subconsciously learning every moment of the day, but the more you participate with that learning process, the more, potentially, you can make of your life. This is because when you understand what you are working with it helps you with the process. You can learn in your own time, through education, reading, humour, and in turn, you will work towards meeting your needs. Tarot and astrology are just two approaches that combine with numerology to help reveal more about the inner you.

Dreams can educate, as they bring to the surface hidden messages, while your waking dreams provide clues as to the kind of life you may like to create for yourself.

ABOVE The numbers in your chart will deduce which minerals you may be attracted to.

In numerology, each number highlights the positive and negative qualities contained within its potential. Everyone chooses how they incorporate these qualities into their lives, and this in turn influences their personal development or learning curve. Knowing what suits you helps you to make the most of your life.

LIFE ON EARTH

****

ABOVE
Chromosomes
have numerological
significance as
creators of life.

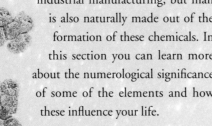

A LL PHYSICAL EXISTENCE throughout the cosmos is made up out of a series of elements. Some are common on earth and others are more common in other areas of the universe. You may identify elements with pharmaceutical or industrial manufacturing, but man is also naturally made out of the formation of these chemicals. In this section you can learn more about the numerological significance of some of the elements and how these influence your life.

GENETICS

There are 23 pairs of human chromosones, each containing a strand of acid called DNA, which transmits genetic information to the cells. There are 46 chromosones and in numerology this number adds up to a 1, which influences the will, free will, and new beginnings and opportunities, making it an open book to life. It also contains the 10, which mirrors the continual process of life and death in rebirth, as humans recreate over and over again. The 4 and the 6 highlight group and personal responsibilities. These numbers show the basic lessons that everyone is learning on earth.

THE ELEMENTS

There are 103 known elements, and some of these substances cannot be made chemically. The 103/13/4 influences growth, transformation, and opportunities, along with responsibility and rebirth. Life is constantly changing and no day is ever the same as the next, which is mirrored in this vibration. Of these 103 elements, 95 occur naturally in nature (with numbers 1 to 95). Again 1 implies infinite potential on the path ahead. The 95 adds up to 14/5, which influences knowledge, will, wisdom, communication, and responsibility.

Contained within these are 81 stable elements. In numerology this number highlights completion and intitiation, as 9 x 9 equals 81. The unstable elements are the numbers 43 and 61, which both add up to 7; this number is a crystalizer of life in its positive potential. These influence humanity by keeping you on your toes so that you learn to find the inner spiritual values. Numbers 84 upward are also unstable elements, and again the 8 and 4 influence responsibility and a need to balance inner spiritual values with outer material values.

ABOVE RIGHT
DNA strands are
the most vital
building blocks.

BELOW All the
elements in the
earth's crust have a
numerological
significance.

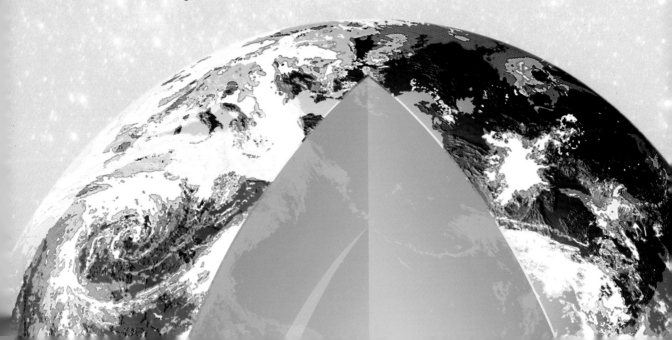

RADIOACTIVE ELEMENTS

The numbers 92 and upward are the radioactive elements, which break down and radiate energy, and some of these elements were created when old stars exploded. Element number 92 is uranium, which adds up to an 11/2, and this number is potentially able to break down all that it needs to create a new path ahead. With a 2 it is constantly doing a balancing act with nature.

Plutonium is element number 94/13/4, which highlights the need for responsibility and can bring great transformation and change, particularly on the physical level.

THE BIG BANG

It is believed that all of life on this planet began many millions of years ago with the Big Bang, or a mass explosion that brought together chemicals which could later form life on earth. This produced hydrogen, element number 1, and helium, element number 2, which is the most common substance found within the universe. The sun is made almost entirely out of these two elements and also gives life to earth.

THE EARTH

The earth supports life in many forms: including those in dimensions of which you may not be consciously aware. About 75 percent of earth's crust is made of oxygen (element number 8) and silicon (element number 14), and bacteria formed 3.5 million years ago and preserved in fossils and rocks. Number 8 for oxygen is one of the most karmic numbers in numerology, and as this book reiterates, karma can teach you about responsibility. Number 14/5, for silicon, contains the qualities of communication, self-expression, motivation, responsibility, and it can be unpredictable.

ABOVE Although we may go around in a world of our own sometimes, we are all a part of a bigger picture.

The element number 26 is iron, which makes up 35 percent of the earth; these numbers add up to an 8, so iron can bring richness to life, by balancing Heaven and earth, spirituality with materialism.

THE EARTH'S ATMOSPHERE

The earth's atmosphere is 75 percent nitrogen, which is element number 7; this number influences the spiritual connection of humanity and supports the materialization of life on earth.

TIME AND CALENDARS

* * * * * * * * * * * * * * * * *

TIME STANDS STILL for no man, woman, or child – a simple truth and a fact of life. Everybody measures time differently. Some people disregard the time, and perhaps follow their own body clocks, and are always late or early for appointments, if they show up at all. Others are time-conscious and live their lives within the confines of each minute or hour of the day.

Timing is also important on earth, as you may like to do things at the right time, or have the philosophy that everything happens in its own time. You may also get "drunk" on time, so that your body is in one place while your mind is effectively elsewhere in time. In some dimensions time cannot be measured; for example, time doesn't exist for a soul.

Calendars are one way of measuring time, but even today some societies and religions disagree about the true time or date, as some use solar calendars while others use lunar calendars, and each offers you a different date of birth and age! The lunar calendar is based upon the moon as it orbits the Earth and a lunar year

ABOVE Elaborate timepieces show people's preoccupation with time.

adds up to approximately 354 days. The Solar Calendar is based on the cycles of the sun and a solar year adds up to approximately 365 days. It makes sure that time is kept precisely.

There are also many different time zones in the world, working from the foundation of Greenwich Mean Time, which is set at zero, and it is interesting to see which countries share the same time zone as yours. All these numbers influence you, but particularly those numbers from your time and date of birth.

Find out the time of day or night when you were born and then consult the number on the 24-hour clock here to see how you may relate to the theme that influences that hour.

THE NUMEROLOGY CLOCK

Midnight to 0100 You may treat each day as completely fresh and new, but you may also view it as a visitor who comes and goes before settling down to a good conversation. You may not connect to it at times.

0100–0200 You may be very aware that you can accomplish goals by a certain time, but you may also try to conquer time too, in which case time sometimes may seem like an enemy.

0200–0300 You may try to weigh up and bargain with time, saying "If you give me more time, I can give you this." You may also measure out your time so that you can balance out your day.

RIGHT A diary helps you allocate your time.

LEFT Ancient lunar calendars can offer you a different date of birth to a solar calendar.

0300–0400 Time may seem to slip through your fingers, perhaps because you are having such a good time. You may not notice time until it's too late, such as missing a train because you didn't look at the clock!

0400–0500 Time may seem like a heavy burden weighing you down at times, while at other times it may seem to support you by giving you time to do practical things and to help you make the most out of your day.

0500–0600 Time may seem to move like a dance: one day this way and one day that, weaving its way through your life. You may dance along, feeling happy to have the opportunity to experience these times.

0600–0700 You may love time like a true friend who gives you the opportunity to live your life fully, supporting you through the difficult times but also enjoying the good times with you.

0700–0800 Time is a great healer of the mind, body, and spirit. Find time to ponder on this for a moment in time, and time's powers may be revealed to you.

LEFT Without monitoring it, time may disappear without you realising.

0800–0900 You may re-evaluate old times over and over again. By going back you may learn to let go of to a certain amount, though you may be wasting time, which can be used to keep you in the here and now.

BELOW A sundial can be a decorative celebration of time-telling.

RIGHT Time is constantly slipping away.

BELOW Time seems to fly when you've got a lot to do.

0900–1000 Egg-timers may fascinate you not only do they let you know when your food is cooked, but they indicate that something is complete. You may particularly fall in line and accept the natural cycles of time.

1000–1100 If you watch your plants and wait for them to grow, time may seem slow and you may get angry or frustrated, but if you focus your attention away, then time may surprise you – giant plants have grown.

1100–Noon Time allows you to aspire to the greatest heights, as you find your own place, your individuality, and your uniqueness in your own time.

Noon–1300 Time is neither looking backward nor forward but is somewhere in the middle; are you in the middle of time? Time lets you make the most of both worlds, the shadow and the light.

1300–1400 Time for transformation; time to take a break; lunchtime in the Western world; siesta time for some; make-or-break time for others. Time is a valuable personal development tool.

1400–1500 Time to get in touch with your inner wisdom; what do you really need to do with your time today? Time may be asking you to communicate and connect with others so that your schedule runs smoothly.

1500–1600 A little light music in the afternoon may mean that you can relax and enjoy time, knowing it is carrying you where you need to go. Time can lighten your load.

BELOW Things can flourish and grow in their own time.

2100–2200 Time to relax; perhaps you can enjoy yourself now that you know another day is almost complete, or you may choose to spend some time educating yourself about all the things people have done with their time throughout history.

LEFT Taking regular breaks may make the day more manageable.

2200–2300 Rest is a time to consolidate your energy and resources and lay the foundations for another new day, which will soon begin. It is time for you to create a sense of harmonious peace for yourself.

1600–1700 Teatime for some, as you take time off for a break. Perhaps you forget that the clock is merrily ticking along, yet it may feel as though you have worked a full day already.

1700–1800 Freedom at last; time to roam around and have some fun, as work is now over for another day (for most people). Perhaps all this time on your hands makes you feel restless. What do you do next with your time?

1800–1900 You may feel like trying to control time, with the end of another day coming into sight. What have you learned? What have you done? Stop the clock, time's running away, though not away from you; time is leading you onward.

1900–2000 You may feel that you play a battle of wills with time, but its will power is always stronger than yours. If you struggle against time, you will always feel that you are getting nowhere. If you really accept that time is stronger than you, then you can feel more triumphant and at one with time.

2000–2100 Time may seem to give and receive simultaneously, but in reality it is indifferent. Your interpretation of time gives it these qualities; perhaps time is teaching you to give and receive.

2300–2400 You may be dreaming as your mind wanders off somewhere else in time, on the great nocturnal adventure. As you sleep, time is waking your subconscious mind to other dimensions – where perhaps time itself does not exist.

ABOVE
"Travellers in Time."

EVENTS IN HISTORY

✦ ✦ ✦ ✦ ✦ ✦ ✦ ✦ ✦ ✦ ✦ ✦ ✦ ✦ ✦

LOOKING THROUGH ANY history book, you can use numerology to help you understand more about events through the ages. You can observe any situation very closely to highlight key issues and lessons that these events were teaching people then and are teaching you now. Every number contained within a specific date is significant, along with the names of people and places associated with these events. Here you can make a brief encounter with a few of the thousands of significant historical dates, including, social, scientific, economic, political, and humanitarian.

ABOVE
Tutankhamun emitted a powerful presence. Perhaps his riches are karmic gifts from the past.

TUTANKHAMUN UNEARTHED

The wonders of ancient Egypt continue to mesmerize people from around the world with their unique mysteries. One of the most fascinating events of relatively recent history, was the unearthing of the 18-year-old Tutankhamun in Egypt, a Pharoah who worshipped Isis. Along with the 143 ornaments and jewels buried with him was a small wreath of white flowers, which had retained its color; it is said to have been placed there by Isis.

Englishman Howard Carter led an expedition up the 16 steps to the burial chamber where Tutankhamun was found 33 centuries after he had been buried. The lid was raised off this precious coffin on February 12 1924, and the Pharoah's bandages were finally unwound on November 11 1925.

RIGHT Neil Armstrong, the first man on the moon, made history.

Numerologically Howard Carter's first Name Number adds up to 33, which is a master number and also the number of centuries since Tutankhamun was buried, so the Egyptologist may have been unconsciously subconsciously drawn toward the pharoah. His Family Name Number, Carter, added up to a 29/11; with all the 1s he had a brilliant mind. Tutankhamun was buried with his 143 ornaments, which adds up to an 8, so his lifetime of great riches may have been a karmic gift. Number 8 influences money and power, and he may have been a strong leader and initiator. The 16/7 steps to his chamber also highlight the spiritual elements.

Carter unearthed the coffin on the 12th day of the month, which highlights completion (the Pharoah's vision was also complete). The whole date adds up to a 30/3, a good day to expand the riches of the mind and be uplifted in the joy of the spirit. When you add up the day and month it becomes 14/5, yet again highlighting inner wisdom and knowledge being communicated to the world.

The Pharoah's bandages were finally taken off in the 11th day of the 11th month; this number influences prophecy, teaching, inspiration, and spirituality. The whole date again adds up to a 39/3, a time to let go of the past and expand into the future.

MAN ON THE MOON

The first man landed on the moon on July 21 1969. The 21/3 highlights expansion, and the whole date adds up to 53/8, so it was man's karma to expand and to move forward on that important day.

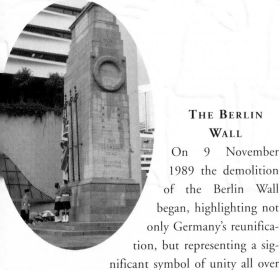

THE BERLIN WALL

On 9 November 1989 the demolition of the Berlin Wall began, highlighting not only Germany's reunification, but representing a significant symbol of unity all over Europe. The day is a 9, which influences endings and new beginnings and humanitarian issues; the 11 influences service to humanity, spirituality, and the break down of situations that stand in the way of progress (with the 1s). 11 was also the sum total of the whole date.

HONG KONG HANDED BACK TO CHINA

Britain handed over Hong Kong to China on July 1 1997. The day was a 1, influencing new directions and a fresh start. The month and the whole day add up to a 7, which highlights the completion of a situation and an alignment with nature.

PERSONAL YEAR EVENTS

The Dalai Lama

The 14th Dalai Lama was born in Tibet on July 6 1935. His Personality Number is a 6, so he was born to be of service to others, and to learn to be generous with his love and kind toward people. Number 6 also highlights a need to be aware of the whole group's needs.

His Life Path Number is a 31/4, a number often associated with Tibet. It highlights the spiritual warrior's relentless determination, a flag-bearer illuminating the needs of others. It also influences a strong spiritual will and natural leadership. This was literally tested on March 31 1959 when the Dalai Lama went into exile in northern India.

The Dalai Lama's first day in India, the 31st, aligns with his 31/4 Life Path Number, which means he was being reminded to follow through on his committment to his work. Indeed this was also reiterated in his Personal Year Number at the time, 36/9, which influences selfless service, humanitarian qualities, compassion, education, and joy.

Martin Luther King Jnr.

Martin Luther King, the civil rights leader, was born on January 15 1929 and was killed in 1968. Martin's interest in social issues may have arisen from the influence of his Personality Number 15/6, and also his two First Names which both added up to 30/3, so politics, social issues, and self-expression played a large part in his life. His Life Path Number, 37/1, influenced his ability to lead.

His Personal Year Number was a 36/9, highlighting humanitarian and social issues. The 9 also signifies an ending and a new beginning; King died in a 38/11 Personal Year, a number highlighting breakthrough.

ABOVE The Dalai Lama teaches compassion for all human beings.

LEFT The handover of Hong Kong to China, July 1 1997. Number 1 highlights new beginnings.

BELOW Martin Luther King, a strong leader who was clearly able to get his message across.

GEOLOGY

YOU CAN LEARN much about the world from the geology of rocks, stones, and crystals, some which have been around for millions of years. Geology has taught us a lot about the origins of our life on this earth.

You are made up of a composition of minerals, and may be attracted to wearing certain minerals because they look beautiful and make you feel good to wear them. Crystals also have healing powers and sometimes you may crave specific foods containing minerals needed by your body. Wearing a crystal can also help to heal you, because they give out energy that influences your whole magnetic field.

There are many different sorts of rocks and minerals and each country may be identified with certain types. They come in the most breath-

ABOVE Minerals from the earth can teach us a great deal about our existence.

taking array of colors, some of which seem so beautiful that it is a privilege to be able to witness this miracle of nature. Some stones and minerals may be exported to other countries, to make into jewelry.

With crystal, the way the stone is cut defines its monetary value. Crystals have two basic shapes: cubic and hexagonal, with the number 6 influencing beauty and wisdom. Emerald, diamond, and gold are known as precious stones or minerals; other minerals include marble, sandstone, quartz, chalk, and slate. Platinum is said to be rarer and more expensive than any other mineral in the world; it adds up to 34/7, which highlights an alignment with nature, or perfection.

Quartz Crystal

MINERALS AND NUMBERS

From the numbers in your chart you can see what kinds of minerals you may be attracted to, and it can also give you a clue as to the physical, emotional, mental, and spiritual levels they may be working on or helping to heal. You can also look up your Personal Year Number to find the minerals you may be attracted to buy in any particular year. It may also help you to decide which minerals to buy as presents for friends, or, even more importantly, for that special person in your life.

1 With a 1 in your chart, you may be attracted to aquamarine, which is found in Brazil, Australia, and Pakistan. It is one of the most desirable and sought-after gemstones in the world. This number is associated with the mind, so perhaps it may help you to focus or concentrate on activities, or you may feel clearer if you are around it or wearing it. The number 1 influences individuality and independence, so perhaps you feel like a rare jewel yourself when you are wearing aquamarine.

Aquamarine

Garnet

2 With a 2 in your chart, you may be attracted to quartz which is found in the United Kingdom or Brazil; garnets from Africa and Sri Lanka; or gold from Canada. They may help you to connect with your feelings, because this number influences your emotions. Perhaps you feel it is easier to open up when you are wearing them, or you may feel that it helps you to feel protected when you may feel vulnerable or sensitive.

Laser Quartz

Herkimore
Diamond

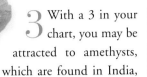

3 With a 3 in your chart, you may be attracted to amethysts, which are found in India, Uruguay, and Brazil; or rubies, from the United States, Tibet, and India. You may like these gemstones because they give you a sense of relaxation, particularly if you wear them or have them close by. These minerals may help to bring out your creativity and help you learn to express yourself. They also look beautiful too.

Amethyst

4 With a 4 in your chart, you may be attracted to silver which is found in Russia and Canada. This mineral works on many levels, but with a 4 it may be reminding you to keep your connection with the ground or to be responsible. Perhaps you like to have lots of silver around to remind you of the Earth, and you may also feel extra-special when you wear it as jewelry.

5 With a 5 in your chart, you may be attracted to rose quartz which is found in America, Madagascar, and Portugal; or to amazonite from Russia. Number 5 influences communication, so you may feel more confident about speaking out when you are close to or wearing these minerals, or you may feel more freedom to express yourself. It may also help you to feel connected to others.

6 With a 6 in your chart, you may find diamonds which are found in China, Russia, Brazil, and Australia, particularly attractive. This number 6 influences your desire to look and feel good, and to find pleasure and joy, and wearing a beautiful diamond may certainly help. You may feel an instinctual bond with jewels as they draw you closer to

the inner beauty of life.

7 With a 7 in your chart, you may be drawn to one of the most precious minerals of all, platinum, which is found in Canada and Russia. Perhaps its rarity is teaching you to appreciate life and the chance you have to be alive. You may also be attracted to pearls from Persia. Number 7 influences illusion, so perhaps these minerals can teach you to look past the material value of life to see the inner spiritual essence mirrored in every mineral.

Opal

8 With an 8 in your chart, you may be attracted to turquoise from Mexico or opals from Brazil. The number 8 influences the mind and wearing or being around these minerals may allow you to feel your connection to your soul. With an 8, you may be assertive and these minerals may help you to connect with the gentle or passive aspects within you. There can be great strength in gentleness, and these minerals may also at times help you to regain your strength.

9 With a 9 in your chart, you may be attracted to the mineral aragonite from Morocco. It looks rich in color, ranging from deep red-brown to black. Black contains all the rays of the spectrum, so wearing this mineral may help you learn to adapt to all the situations you may face in life, or to get along with many different types of people. It may also help you to connect with your spirituality.

Amazonite

SYMBOLS, GEOMETRY, AND SHAPES

* * * * * * * * * * * * * * * * * *

ALL SHAPES AND form can be translated into numbers and can therefore reveal hidden information. For example, a mirror may be represented in the number 7, because it is mirroring back the true or real you (qualities contained within its potential) or what you physically look like. The number 7 also influences introspection and personal development, where you look at yourself from within. In life it is said that people mirror each other too and also that the external life mirrors the internal process of life, whether that of an individual or the whole of humanity. A mirror is therefore one of the most powerful symbols.

ABOVE The mirror symbolises your ability to see yourself as you are. The truth is revealed.

Symbols and shapes are also powerful, which is why at the office you may not like to sit near the pointed edge of a cupboard or a metal radiator. Perhaps the corner of the cupboard is reminding you of the sharp edge of life and the metal heater is reminding you of coldness, or if it is piping hot it may may mean that you feel emotionally smothered by its intense heat. You are, however, surrounded by shapes and symbols every moment of the day, and you will be attracted to certain symbols based on the influence of the numbers in your chart. For example, you may have an 8 personality and like clinging clothes to show off your body shape.

Symbols have different meanings for different people, and your interpretation may also change, depending on your mood or mental attitude. The ideas behind the form or symbol are most significant for the impressions they make upon you as they penetrate your deepest subconscious mind and your emotions. Many symbols have meanings passed down from past generations, like cultural symbols from different countries around the world. For example, in India an elephant is considered to represent good fortune and a cow is a sacred symbol. In numerology your Karma Number particularly represents influences from the past lives and your Soul Number may also bring back certain memories.

French culture had a literary movement based on symbolism, in vogue at the end of the late 19th century, when it was believed that poetry should relate to the moral and physical representations of certain symbols. In numerology the 19th century highlights the number 1 and 9, numbers that both influence innovation; the 9 also has the quality of morals contained within its potential.

Symbols have the power to heal or to create disharmony within their environment. They are very powerful objects to try and take control of, which is why many people spend money investing in an interior designer or feng shui consultant, who brings in energies harmonious with those people who are living there. You can do something like this yourself by observing the major numbers in your chart, and introducing objects to bring out these qualities.

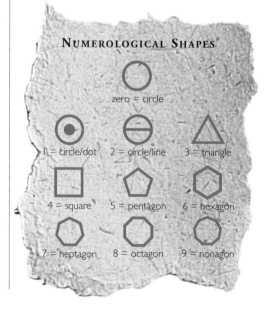

NUMEROLOGICAL SHAPES

zero = circle

1 = circle/dot   2 = circle/line   3 = triangle

4 = square   5 = pentagon   6 = hexagon

7 = heptagon   8 = octagon   9 = nonagon

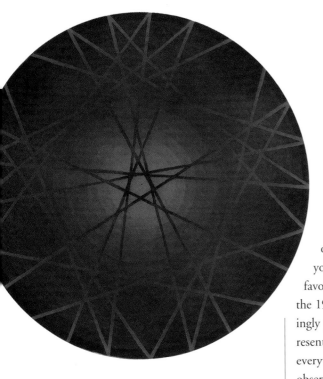

SYMBOLS AND NUMBERS

0	CIRCLE	*infinity*
1	SEEDS	*new beginnings*
2	WATER	*emotions*
3	PAINTING	*joy*
4	EARTH	*provider*
5	TRAIN	*adventure*
6	BOWL	*nurturing*
7	TREE	*life, fertility*
8	URN	*life, death, rebirth*
9	FIRE	*purification*

GEOMETRY

Geometry is based on shapes. Pythagoras, who was also a mathematician as well as numerologist, invented his own methods using shapes, such as his famous theorem based on a right-angled triangle. Geometrical shapes have also been popularly used around the world as ways of estimating, for example, the amount of grain contained within a stockpile, or the number of people in a crowd.

One of the most basic shapes in the universe is that of the circle, which represents an 0. It is likely the collective influence will be stronger than your own in interpreting its

shape; you can interpret this and other geometrical shapes in your own way by stepping out of the compulsive conditioning which may be influencing you.

Geometry is the visual understanding of numbers through shape and form, and you will see that each generation has its favorite symbols and shapes. For example, in the 1960s in England the Mini car was exceedingly popular, and its shape was rounded, a representation of the 6 in the 60s. Indeed everything goes in cycles and trends, and by observing numbers in life you can understand why some are popular, and when they may potentially be popular shapes too. Of course each country has its own national and regional shapes and by simply looking around you where you live, or as you travel, you may be able to see which numbers are also influencing you.

Geometry also contains different elements of yin and yang. For example, yang, an active energy, influences the numbers 1, 3, 5, 7, and 9, while the passive or receptive energy of yin influences the numbers 2, 4, 6, and 8. In the 60s, the Mini car and miniskirt highlighted a feminine and receptive energy, which was reflected in many other products and the openness of designs of the time. These numbers are also contained within your own Numerology chart, and your major numbers in particular can highlight the kinds of shapes which may appeal to you.

Each of the Personal Years, as well as the monthly, weekly, and daily number vibrations, can also have an influence over the kinds of shapes you may enjoy or bring into your environment. It may also explain why you may suddenly get restless or bored with certain shapes of items around your dwelling, and want to remove them.

ABOVE The ancient Greeks adapted geometry in their architecture, making esthetic use of numbers.

ABOVE LEFT *"Carbonisation."* The five-pointed star represents human life, and the intense fiery heat represents spirit.

BELOW An icon of the 60s, the Mini epitomized the relaxed feel of that time.

ART

* * * * * * * * * * * * * * * * * * *

ART HAS MANY different meanings, interpretations, and styles, including forms that have yet to be invented. It may be expressed through painting, photography, or sculpture. Here you can find out more about the types of pictorial art that may attract you, whether through colors, mood, structure, or scenes they depict. Also you may find out how you express your artistic creativity, based on the influence of the major numbers in your chart or your Personal Year Number. You can also find out more about three popular artists, Pablo Picasso, Leonardo Da Vinci, and Claude Monet, identifying some of their numerological traits.

ABOVE Sketching a simple charcoal drawing expresses your creativity.

ART STYLES AND METHODS WITH NUMEROLOGY

1 With a 1 in your chart, you may like to put energy and vitality into your paintings and artwork. Perhaps your creations seem loud, wild, and bold as they step off the canvas and grab people's attention. You may be mindful about what you paint, and spend a great deal of time thinking about what you wish to achieve with your paintings before you even start. You may resist beginning until you feel the right moment, when the force of your mental focus drives it through.

Salvador Dali may be one of your favorite painters. He had original flair and imagination, and his surrealistic paintings often took a symbolic view of life. You may also be drawn to Dali's extreme originality, and to his bright, eccentric mind. He was a genius in his field and you may be attracted to this energy.

2 With a 2 in your chart, you may be drawn toward painting watercolours, which are sometimes delicate, soft, and gentle and may help you to connect with your feelings. At other times you may channel all your unexpressed emotions into your work and they may seem complex. Perhaps you like to paint watery scenes too, such as lakes, waterfalls, rivers, or even rainstorms. You may enjoy creating simple scenes and have a knack of being able to capture the mood of the day brilliantly.

You may be attracted to creative masterpieces by Paul Gauguin, with their beautiful colors and the flair with which he used them. Indeed the colors of his paintings may sometimes attract you more than their actual design.

3 With a 3 in your chart, you may be abundantly creative and artistic and have a gift with your hands. You may enjoy painting in many different styles and colors, and you like the freedom to paint without the confines of doing the "right" thing or having to follow a certain method of design. You may be talented, with an ability to paint according to whatever is required, and to feel joy about your creations. Your paintings may be inspirational whether you are a trained artist or have had no formal training at all.

Michelangelo may be one of your favorite painters for his awe-inspiring frescoes, particularly in the Sistine Chapel in Rome. This may result from an interest in religion and spirituality, qualities contained within the potential of the number 3.

4 With a 4 in your chart, you may enjoy creating black and white sketches as much as painting in oils on canvas. You may also relish the planning as much as the execution. You may enjoy creating structured work, and like to keep to a technique that is reliable and practical for the style you choose.

Thomas Gainsborough, a landscape artist, may be one of your favorite painters. Some of his work looked dark and dramatic, one of the qualities contained within the 4.

ABOVE *"Butterfly Light."* Light dancing.

5 With a 5 in your chart, you may love to paint in vibrant and bright colors, which lift you up and make you feel alive. You may love painting even if you are not particularly skilled. You may enjoy painting scenes of the people around you, or of different places you have visited. You may also be changeable, and experiment with different styles of paintings.

You may identify with Leonardo Da Vinci's trait of leaving paintings unfinished, a quality contained within the potential of the 5.

PABLO PICASSO

1881–1973

Picasso was a prolific creator of art, as well as a sculptor, designer, and a graphic artist. He was incredibly versatile and was able to easily adapt to the moment. It is said that he did not think in terms of past, present, and future, but expressed himself in his own space and time.

Picasso caused a revolution in art in the 20th century with his then unusual designs. He developed a style called Cubism, while also designing ballet costumes, and producing surreal works of art.

Picasso's First and Family Name Numbers both add up to a 1, and both have sub-influences of the 10, therefore he was born to lead and to find his own direction in life, to stamp his own individuality upon his works and channel his numerous ideas into his creative expression. Pablo's Life Path Number adds up to 53 or 8, and it was the 5 and 3 that were encouraging him to communicate his knowledge

to the world and the 8 that highlighted his spiritual strength and will. He painted his first major works in 1895, which adds up to a 23 (or 5), when he was aged 14 (or 5). This highlights soul energy infusing into his mind, helping to bring out his inner wisdom and knowledge. Picasso's Personality Number was a 25/7, which explains his speedy materialization of work – a prolific 20,000 creations in his time.

RIGHT Picasso's important numbers show he was meant to break the mold.

CLAUDE MONET
1840–1926

Monet was a French impressionist who delighted in the perfection of his creative works. He sometimes painted the same series of pictures at different times during the day until the "perfect" result was achieved. Monet painted in pastel colors, and his sensitivity to life shone through his paintings; he was also a fine caricaturist. His creative output was prolific; he produced around 25,000 paintings, drawings, and pastels, some of which radically altered the perception of art at that time. Some of Monet's most famous masterpieces were *Haystacks* (1889–93), *Rouen Cathedral* (1892–94), and *Water Lilies* (1899–06).

Claude's first name adds up to a 19, or a 1, therefore he had the potential to be able to break down people's perceptions about art. Many great inventors have a major number as a 1, as they are directed by the focus and will to produce their ideas into form. Indeed Claude started working on the great *Rouen Cathedral* in 1891, which adds up to a 1 (a new beginning), and its title also adds up to a 19 or 1, which was Monet's Goal Number, too. Monet, his Family Name, adds up to a 22 or 4, a master number that gave him his interest in watercolors and pastel colors associated with the emotions, as well as his acute sensitivity. He was born in 1840, which also adds up to a 4, which helped Monet to bring his ideas down to earth.

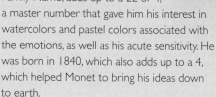

LEFT Monet was a prolific creator of art and often painted many versions of the same scene.

6 With a 6 in your chart, you may love to paint in rich colors that highlight the sensuality of the scene. You may enjoy painting food, flowers, cafés, or sensual love scenes. You may like your paintings to make you feel good, and look as if you can reach out and touch them. Perhaps you also enjoy painting harmonious scenes, or ones that reveal some of the less glamorous sides of life.

Henri Matisse was a colorful and versatile painter who may be one of your favorite painters. You can literally touch some of the people in his art, because he was a sculptor, too.

7 With a 7 in your chart, you may love to sit and absorb yourself in painting, as it gives you quiet time to introspect and connect with your inner self. You may enjoy painting spiritual or religious scenes, or buildings or places of interest such as the 7 Wonders of the World. Perhaps you make charcoal etchings, or spend a great deal of time laboring over a watercolor until it is just right. You may like to pay great attention to technical detail and ensure that each work of art is as perfect as possible.

Claude Monet, the French impressionist who at times sacrificed all for the final results of perfection of his masterpieces, may be one of your favorite artists.

8 With an 8 in your chart, you may like to paint powerful pictures showing strength of character and your ability to create. Perhaps you paint in bright and strong colors such as red and black, or in oils, where the depth and richness of the colors feel strong and powerful. You may at times be able to reach deep into your inner self to connect with your spirituality. Sketching scenes in black and white may also interest you.

Vincent Van Gogh, the Dutch impressionist who led a tortured life, may appeal, as a result of the power of the colors he used and his inner spiritual strength.

9 With a 9 in your chart, you may love to paint in loud or garish colors that express your sometimes liberal attitude toward life. You may have a gift for art and be open to every kind of style and form, as you can see the light in them all. Perhaps you are naturally inventive with your work and can conjure up new ways of depicting a scene; even a cat on a mat may be drawn in an abstract or unusual way. You may also experiment with color.

The Spanish painter and sculptor Pablo Picasso may be one of your favorite artists. His inventive nature helped to transform the field of art in his time.

LEONARDO DA VINCI

1452–1519

Leonardo Da Vinci was a Florentine artist who was one of the masters of the Renaissance movement that influenced Italy from the 14th to the 16th centuries. It injected fresh energy into art and precipitated a rebirth of Classical principles. Leonardo was said to believe that beauty was not found in the correct technique of a painting, but its overall content. He painted many masterpieces, but was reknowned for leaving his artistic creations incomplete, and his style often used dark colors. Some of his most famous works include a fresco of the *The Last Supper* (c. 1495), *Mona Lisa* (1503), and *St John the Baptist* (c.1515).

Leonardo's First Name or Goal Number adds up to a 39, or 3, which explains his interest in spiritual and religious paintings and also highlights his artistic gift with his hands. He may have also been a deep thinker; if you look at Mona Lisa and her intelligent eyes, you can see this aspect. Its title adds up to a 30, or 3, too. Da Vinci, his Family Name, adds up to a 35 or 8; coupled with Life Path Number 31, or 4, it explains why many of his paintings looked serious and were painted in dark, mysterious colors. Leonardo's love of beauty and art in any form came from his Personality Number 15 or 6, and it was in 1515 that he painted his masterpiece *St John the Baptist*.

RIGHT Da Vinci's highly cerebral nature shone through his paintings.

AFTERWORD

* * * * * * * * * * * * * * * * * * *

Reading this book you can see that numerology truly mirrors back all aspects of life to you and the whole of life can be explored using this wonderful tool. Indeed there is a diversity of subjects which have been touched upon – each one could be a whole book in itself – and by applying numerology to the subject matter it can teach you even more. Life is constantly evolving and therefore your outlook on various subjects may change too, as you look at life with a different perspective each day. Numerology is therefore a living science.

This book has taken you on an inner journey of discovery, particularly in the chapters concerned with the Personality, Life Path, Soul, Childhood, and Karma Numbers, which highlight the key strengths, challenges and your potential, from your date of birth and names. These numbers hold the key to your health, career, relationships, and the kinds of experiences you may have in your life. You have also been taken on an outer journey to discover more about the world around you, and of course everything you read or experience can teach you more about yourself and about life, for example, historical events, art, music, and medicines.

Each of the numbers 1 to 9 help to simplify the complexities surrounding life, and enable us to grasp the simple messages that life tries to bring to our attention. Essentially, numerology is a practical tool which can provide clarity any moment of the day. *The Complete Illustrated Guide* has shown you how to apply numerology to a vast array of situations in life. There is a bounty of information to be absorbed in this book, but each person interprets life in their own unique way and is guided by his or her own wisdom and perception of truth. Numerology is a wonderful way to help you develop your intuition, as the digits take you deep into your subconcious and bring hidden information to your awareness. Numbers trigger memories from the past, from patterns of behavior or situations, which may be either personal or collective. Numbers repeat themselves in life so that you take notice of them and by simply teaching yourself to observe the cycles 1 to 9, you can make the most of the ebb and flow of life.

Responsibility is the key issue for planet earth and learning more about yourself and how to relate to others and to the world may help you to become even more aware of your own personal responsibility. Pulling together to work on issues collectively may have a powerful influence on your own life, too.

Finally, numerology is fun to use, it is easy to apply, and can be useful in many ways. Life is for learning and if you have a yearning to know more, additional information on the subject is readily accessible. If you feel inspired to pursue a more in-depth exploration of numerology, there are many workshops or professional training available (see list of professional contacts on page 185). Enjoy the numbers!

USEFUL ADDRESSES

* * * * * * * * * * * * * * * * * * *

ASSOCIATIONS AND SCHOOLS

If you would like to contact a numerology school or association to learn more about professional training and workshops or to find a professional Numerologist for a chart reading, please send an stamped addressed envelope or international reply coupon to:

UNITED KINGDOM

Association Internationale de
Numerologues (A. I. N.)
8 Melbourn Street
ROYSTON
SG8 7BZ
Hertfordshire

http//www.numerology.org.uk

Connaissance School of Numerology
Royston Cave, Art and Book Shop
8 Melbourn Street
ROYSTON
SG8 7BZ
Hertfordshire

USA

Marina D. Graham
Suite 200
888 Prospect Street
La Jolla
CA 92037

FRANCE

Christian Gilles School
Residence de L'Abbey Royle
17 Rue Pirel
93200 Saint Denis
PARIS

AUSTRALIA

Character Analysis and Numerology
Mrs C. Anschutz
23 Flinders Street
KENT TOWN
5067
South Australia

NEW ZEALAND

Francie Williams
North Shore Parapsychology School
60 East Coast Bay Road
MILFORD
New Zealand

FURTHER READING

* * * * * * * * * * * * * * * * * *

RODFORD BARRATT, *The Elements Of Numerology* (Element Books, UK, 1994)
This book gives overall information about the Personality Number, the Life Path Number and about the influence of your names. What is particularly appealing is that the author gives information for every single letter in the alphabet and chronicles how to choose a name. It is easy to read and a very practical book.

JOHN BERGES, *The Sacred Vessel Of The Mysteries*, (Planetwork Press, USA, 1998)
This esoteric numerology book focuses on the power of Numerology in prayer and meditation, specifically in relation to the Great Invocation mantra which is a universal prayer for all religions. The book highlights the Pythagorean method of numerology and the numbers 1 to 10, and includes information on Isis, Egypt, ancient Greece and the teachings of Tibetan master Djwhal Khul.

FAITH JAVANE AND DUSTY BUNKER, *Numerology and the Divine Triangle*, (Whitford Press, USA, 1979)
This book offers in-depth information about numerology from your whole date of birth and from your names. Its primary focus is on the numbers 1 to 81, along with corresponding information on the tarot and astrology.

INDEX

✶✶✶✶✶✶✶✶✶✶✶✶✶✶✶✶✶✶